S0-CFT-585

THE DOGMATIC CONSTITUTION ON DIVINE REVELATION

De Divina Revelatione

THE
DOGMATIC CONSTITUTION
ON
DIVINE REVELATION
OF
VATICAN COUNCIL II

Promulgated by Pope Paul VI
November 18, 1965

Commentary and Translation

by

George H. Tavard, A.A.

1966
VATICAN II DOCUMENTS
PAULIST PRESS
(Paulist Fathers)
Glen Rock, N.J.

Nihil Obstat:
Rev. James J. O'Connor
Censor Librorum

Imprimatur:
✠Leo A. Pursley, D.D.
Bishop of Fort Wayne-South Bend
January 30, 1966

The Nihil Obstat and Imprimatur are official declarations that a book or pamphlet is free of doctrinal or moral error. No implication is contained therein that those who have granted the Nihil Obstat and Imprimatur agree with the contents, opinions or statements expressed.

Library of Congress
Catalog Card Number: 66-19148

Cover Design: Claude Ponsot

Published by Paulist Press

Editorial Office: 304 W. 58th St., N.Y., N.Y. 10019
Business Office: Glen Rock, New Jersey 07452

Printed in the
United States of America
by Our Sunday Visitor Press

Contents

COMMENTARY by George H. Tavard, A.A. 7

I Pre-history of the Constitution 7

II History of the Constitution 11

III The Plan of the Constitution 17

IV Some Theological Problems 23

V The Constitution on Divine Revelation in the Council's Work 50

VI Ecumenical Importance of the Constitution 52

THE DOGMATIC CONSTITUTION ON DIVINE REVELATION 55

Prologue 57

I Revelation 58
Study-Club Questions 62

II The Transmission of Divine Revelation 64
Study-Club Questions 69

III Holy Scripture: Divine Inspiration and Interpretation 71
Study-Club Questions 75

IV The Old Testament 77
Study-Club Questions 79

V The New Testament 81
Study-Club Questions 84

VI Holy Scripture in the Church's Life 86
Study-Club Questions 91

SELECTED BIBLIOGRAPHY 93

Commentary

I
Pre-history of the Constitution

The last two Ecumenical Councils before Vatican Council II pronounced on the topic of the present Constitution, which should therefore be read in the light of these previous pronouncements: it establishes a new milestone along the way pointed out by the Council of Trent and Vatican Council I for theological reflection concerning the nature of revelation and man's means of perceiving it.

The Council of Trent, at its beginning, was eager to establish clearly what doctrinal basis it would take in order to examine the questions raised by the Protestant Reformation. Accordingly, its 3rd session (February, 1546) re-endorsed the Creed of Nicaea-Constantinople as the traditional formulation of faith. And the 4th session (April, 1546) defined the Council's attitude to the apostolic traditions and to the Holy Scriptures. The essential part of this decree should be quoted so that readers of the *Constitution on Divine Revelation* of Vatican Council II can refer to it:

". . . keeping this always in view, that, errors being removed, there may be preserved in the Church the purity of the Gospel, which, after it was formerly promised through the prophets in the Holy Scriptures, our Lord Jesus Christ, the Son of God, first promulgated personally, then through his apostles ordered to be preached to every creature as the source of all saving truth and moral discipline—perceiving also that this truth and discipline is contained in written books and in unwritten traditions which have reached down to us, having been received by the apostles from Christ's own mouth or transmitted as though by hand by the same apostles under the dictation of the Holy Spirit—following the example of the orthodox Fathers, (the Council) receives and venerates with an equal attitude of piety and an equal reverence all the books of the Old and the New Testaments, since the one God is the author of both, and also the traditions themselves, pertaining to faith and to mores, as coming from Christ himself orally or from the Holy Spirit, and kept in the Catholic Church by continuous succession . . ." [1]

After stating this principle, the Council of Trent listed all the books of the Old and the New Testaments and, in a complementary decree, explained how these Holy Scriptures were to be interpreted.

On January 6, 1870, at the end of its 3rd session, Vatican Council I promulgated the Constitution *Dei Filius*, which dealt with revelation and faith. After a first chapter stating briefly the doctrine of creation, the second chapter explained revelation, which

[1] *D.S.* (*Denzinger-Schönmetzer*), n. 1501.

in turn led to the third chapter on faith, and to the final chapter on the relations between faith and reason. Revelation, as explained in chapter 2, implies the natural cognoscibility of God as the principle and the end of all creation. To this natural knowledge, God, out of his infinite goodness, has added a supernatural revelation, by which he may be known "rapidly, with firm certainty and without error". "This supernatural revelation, according to the faith of the universal Church as declared by the Council of Trent, is contained in written books and in unwritten traditions which have reached down to us, having been received by the apostles from Christ's own mouth or transmitted as though by hand by the same apostles under the dictation of the Holy Spirit."[2] There followed an endorsement of the Tridentine Canon of the Bible and of the principle established by Trent for the interpretation of Scripture.

The statement of Trent was occasioned by the crisis of the Reformation; that of Vatican Council I was part of the Council's attempt to stem the tide of Rationalism, which, at the end of the century, was to lead to the rise of Modernism and the ensuing controversies, to the encyclical *Pascendi* (1907), to the oath against Modernism and to a series of cautious decrees of the Biblical Commission on the interpretation of the Bible.

When Vatican Council II began in 1962, no new crisis made it necessary to prepare a document on Scripture with a polemical edge. Especially since the recent development of Bultmann's school of interpretation, some controversies about the exegesis of the New Testament had taken place both among

---

2 *D.S.*, n. 3006.

Protestants and among Catholics, yet they had not reached the point where an intervention by the supreme magisterium would become urgent. On the contrary, since the encyclical of Pius XII, *Divino afflante Spiritu* (1943), modern Catholic exegesis had developed in peace with all the scientific tools at its disposal. Discussions on the meaning of the Bible, focused on the concept of *sensus plenior*, had taken place, and the traditional idea that God in the Bible said more than the human authors knew, was thus able to find its place in the relatively new context of scientific exegesis.

In the field of historical scholarship, the renewed study of the decrees of the Council of Trent, which had been made possible by the publication of the Acts and Diaries of the Council by the "Görres Society" in the last century, had drawn attention to the exact meaning of the decree of April, 1546. In the light of modern research, which had been anticipated by many previous authors, it became clear that the Council of Trent had not intended to divide revelation into two distinct, partial and independent sources, Scripture and Tradition, but rather that it wished primarily to express the unity of both in their common source, the Gospel. Debates on this point were at times sharp, but they never endangered any point of faith and therefore did not require a final decision by the magisterium.

Under these conditions, why should Vatican Council II promulgate a special Constitution *De Divina Revelatione?* The motivation may appear better after a short survey of the history of the present Constitution.

II

History of the Constitution

The Preparatory Theological Commission presented a "schema", entitled *De Fontibus Revelatonis* (*On the Sources of Revelation*) to the first session of the Council. This was part of a series of schemas (*On the Preservation of the Deposit of Faith in Its Purity; On Christian Moral Order; On Chastity, Marriage, the Family and Virginity; On the Church; On the Blessed Virgin Mary*) destined to strengthen present-day Catholic doctrine by stating it authoritatively and putting an end to theological debates. Had these projects been accepted by the Council in the form in which they were originally presented, they would have hardened Catholic theology and would have made Vatican Council II a ghetto Council reinforcing the Church's isolation rather than her renovation and spirit of *aggiornamento*.

The schema "On the Sources of Revelation" had five chapters:

I. The Double Source of Revelation

II. The Inspiration, Inerrancy and Literary Form of Scripture

III. The Old Testament

IV. The New Testament

V. Holy Scripture in the Church

Debate on this schema (Text I) began on November 14, 1962, and ended on November 21. The discussion was severely critical of the text, and there was sharp disagreement among the bishops on its value as a basis for a conciliar document. A vote was taken on November 20 to answer the question: "Must discussion of this schema end now?"; and the division was as follows: 1368 *yes;* 822 *no;* 19 votes were *null.* As the required two-thirds majority had not been reached, discussion was to continue. On November 21, however, Pope John's decision was announced: he appointed a special commission to rewrite the schema and present it again to the Council in a way that would be acceptable to the majority.

The second schema on the question, entitled *De Divina Revelatione* (*On Divine Revelation*) and prepared by this mixed Commission, was sent to the bishops before the second session of the Council (September-November, 1963). This schema (Text II) had the following structure:

Prologue
I. The Revealed Word of God
II. The Divine Inspiration and the Interpretation of Sacred Scripture
III. The Old Testament
IV. The New Testament
V. The Use of Sacred Scripture in the Church

This second version of the schema was never debated in the Council. In his address at the end of the 2nd session, Pope Paul VI noted this fact and listed the question of revelation among those that still had to be treated or, in his own words, that "remained open to ulterior study and discussion". Paul VI added: "We hope that these will be led to a good end in the course of the third session." He then mentioned the problem of revelation in these words:

> "Such is, for instance, the case with the question concerning divine revelation. The Council will answer it in such a way as to safeguard the sacred deposit of divine truth from

> the errors, abuses and doubts which threaten its subjective value, and at the same time to give a just orientation to the biblical, patristic and theological studies which Catholic scholars will strive to promote with trust, zeal and wisdom, in fidelity to the Church's magisterium and with the help of all the serious conclusions of modern science."

Upon reception of this new schema, however, many bishops had sent their remarks to the Doctrinal Commission of the Council, so that a revision was possible in the light of these written communications. Accordingly, the Doctrinal Commission revised the text, thus producing a third version, which was sent to the bishops before the third session of the Council (September-November, 1964), after being approved by letter (May 30, 1964) by the President and the Secretary of the Secretariat for Christian Unity, representing one-half of Pope John's mixed Commission. This version (Text III) was finally discussed at the third session (September 30-October 6, 1964).

In keeping with the working methods followed by the Council, a revision of Text III was then made in the light of the debate, in which account was taken of both the speeches pronounced in the General Congregations and the letters sent in by the bishops. This revision made by the Council's Doctrinal Commission resulted in a fourth text (Text IV), which differed only slightly from Text III. Both of these had the following structure:

Prologue

I. Revelation Itself

II. The Transmission of Divine Revelation

III. The Divine Inspiration and the Interpretation of Holy Scripture

IV. The Old Testament
V. The New Testament
VI. Holy Scripture in the Church's Life

Text IV was brought to the voting stage during the fourth session. The twenty votes that were required took place from September 20-24, 1965. The most important, namely, the general votes on each chapter, deserve to be recorded:

Chapter I
placet (yes) 1822
non placet (no) 3
placet juxta modum (yes, with a written reservation) .. 248
void 6

Chapter II
placet 1874
non placet 9
placet juxta modum 354
void 9

Chapter III
placet 1777
non placet 6
placet juxta modum 324

Chapter IV
placet 2183
non placet 0
placet juxta modum 47
void 3

Chapter V
placet 1850
non placet 4
placet juxta modum 313
void 3

Chapter VI
placet 1915
non placet 1
placet juxta modum 212
void 4

The Doctrinal Commission proceeded next to the definitive revision in the light of the reservations expressed in the votes *placet juxta modum.* The result (Text V) was adopted by the Council on October 29, 1965 with the following votes:

Chapter I		Chapter IV	
placet	2169	*placet*	2178
non placet	23	*non placet*	8
void	2	void	2

Chapter II		Chapter V	
placet	2123	*placet*	2115
non placet	55	*non placet*	19
void	7	void	5

Chapter III		Chapter VI	
placet	2154	*placet*	2126
non placet	31	*non placet*	14
void	4	void	6

The vote on the entire text was as follows:

placet	2081
non placet	27
void	7

The final vote covering the whole document took place on November 18:

placet	2344
non placet	6

The Constitution was promulgated by Pope Paul on the same day.

A comparison of the successive forms of the document on revelation shows that the revisions were made in three directions:

In the first place, an explanation of the fact and the notion of revelation, which had not been introduced in Text I, was added and developed in the successive revisions. It became a prologue in Text II, and the first chapter in Texts III, IV, and V.

In the second place, the explanation of Scripture and its relations to Tradition became less and less controversial. Whereas the first text adopted one particular interpretation of Tradition (as a partial source of faith, complementary to, and independent of, Scripture), the subsequent texts did not take sides among theologians in the controverted question of the quantitative extension of Scripture and of Tradition: they left it open for theology to hold that the entire revelation is in Scripture and also in Tradition, or that only a part of revelation is in Scripture while all of it is in Tradition, or even, as with Text I, that a part of revelation is in Scripture and another part in Tradition alone.

In the third place, the description of controverted questions on the nature of biblical inspiration and on the methods of scientific exegesis became more aware of modern requirements and less inclined to take sides among contending exegetical methods.

The purpose of this conciliar Constitution is to be assessed, as its history clearly shows, less in the light of the polemical implications of the text originally prepared, than in the perspective in which the successive revisions were made, guided as they were by the conciliar debates and by the instructions given by Pope John to the mixed Commission that he created. These revisions made the text eminently pastoral, open to contemporary theology, permissive of theological plurality on controversial matters, and highly encouraging to the researches of exegetes on the interpretation of Scripture and of theologians on the nature of Tradition.

III

The Plan of the Constitution

The plan of the Constitution is not merely a matter of organization; it is mainly one of doctrine. The Constitution begins with a chapter on revelation and ends with one on Scripture in the life of the Church. Its entire purpose is precisely to show how revelation, given once for all in Jesus Christ to mankind as a whole, becomes life in the Church for all those who, by baptism, have been incorporated into Christ. In other words, revelation is neither essentially a doctrine, although it implies one; nor a set of propositions and formulations to be believed, although it may be partially expressed in such propositions; nor the promulgation of an ethical law of prescriptions and proscriptions, although it also implies judgment of the morality of human behavior. Essentially, revelation is a life. It is the very life of God imparted to man through the incarnation of the Son; it is the communication of God's Word understood by man in the Holy Spirit. Thus the first and the last chapters of the Constitution constitute the general framework of the document and of the doctrine it teaches. The first explains how God reveals himself; the last shows how Christians may develop the life of God in themselves by better following the mind of God as shown in the Holy Scriptures. God comes to us as a spoken Word which has resounded temporally upon earth after resounding eternally in God himself; and he is to be perceived through the words of the Scriptures.

Between revelation and the place and use of Scripture for spiritual life in the Church in general and in Christians in particular, the Council has placed several chapters of a somewhat more technical character. Revelation was given through the Word, speaking to the patriarchs and the prophets of the Old Testament, and himself made flesh in Jesus the Savior. But this revelation was meant to reach all men, and not only those who, like St. John, were able to testify: "That which was from the beginning, which we have heard, which we have seen with our own eyes, which we have beheld, which our hands have touched of the Word of life—for the life was manifested; we have seen it, we testify to it, and we announce to you this eternal Life which was with the Father and has appeared to us—that which we have seen and heard, we announce to you, that you also may have communion with us."[3] Revelation reached the apostles directly so that they could bear witness to the light they had seen; it has to reach those coming after the apostles through the testimony of the apostles themselves, the only qualified eyewitnesses.

How revelation reaches the believers after the time of the apostles forms the topic of chapter II: it is transmitted in a Tradition (the word "tradition" means "transmission") channeled down the ages and carried to the ends of the earth in a double movement, spread in space by missionary expansion and preserved in time by historical succession. When it is preached by the apostles and their successors, revelation becomes the Gospel, that is, the "good news", the "glad tidings" of salvation. This Good News, orally communicated by the apostles, was also written down in the Scriptures of the New Testament, which embody the apostolic tradition of the Christian covenant, as the Scriptures

---

[3] I John 1, 1-3.

of the Old Testament embodied the patriarchal and prophetic tradition of the Mosaic covenant. The Holy Spirit is active both in the verbal transmission of the Good News and in the writing, the preservation and the interpretation of the Scriptures. For the Church's indefectibility is at stake in all these actions: she must be able to safeguard fidelity to the doctrine once received, and she must also be in a position to discern the mind of the Spirit when she reads the holy books. Therefore, she is assisted, though in different ways, by the grace of the Holy Spirit, who was sent, as Jesus promised, in order to "guide you into all the truth".[4]

The logic of this line of thought leads naturally to the third chapter, where the inspiration and the interpretation of Scripture are explained. These two concepts go together in theology, as they primarily go together in the experience of those who are familiar with the spiritual reading of the Word of God. Inspiration is the process by which the Spirit took part in the writing down of Scripture, penetrating the minds of its human authors, expressing his purposes through their human conceptions, ideas, hopes, dreams, interpretations of, and reflections upon, the events of their times or of the past. Interpretation is the corresponding process of reading, by which the Church and her members endeavor to read the mind of the Spirit in the writings composed under his inspiration. Since inspiration was granted to individual men for the sake of the Holy People, whose divine calling it was destined to record in the ups and downs of the People's pilgrimage on earth, interpretation must also be made for the sake of the Holy People gathered into the Church under the new covenant.

[4] John 16, 13.

Although it has to be worked out by individual men using the human resources of their talents and scholarship, these men must pursue a purpose that is infinitely larger than they themselves can ever be: the Church's own purpose of communicating with the Father through the real Word understood in the Spirit. They are at the service of the People of God, sensing the mind of the holy community in its permanent encounter with the spoken Word of Tradition and the written Word of Scripture, thereby helping the Church in prophetic anticipations to discover its own faith, and thus contributing their share to the development of doctrine, to the continuation and enlargement of the divine Tradition.

It follows that certain rules must exist for the guidance of experts, exegetes, theologians and preachers in their function of translating the Bible in the language of contemporary men. Exegetes try to discern the meaning of the texts with the scientific tools of history, archaeology, philology, linguistics, comparative religion, hermeneutics; theologians, who need not be different persons, try to interpret the result of exegesis in the context of the analogy of faith and in the continuity of the Church's Tradition; preachers, who of course may also be exegetes and theologians, try to formulate this in the language of the pulpit and to make the written Word which they have understood, a spoken Word through which their hearers may be grasped by the power of the apostolic kerygma.

Accordingly, the third chapter includes several references to the principles of hermeneutics, or interpretation of the Old and New Testaments. The passage explaining these points must be read in the context of contemporary exegetical practice and methods, and in the line of recent pontifical documents regarding problems of exegesis, that is, mainly of Pius XII's encyclical *Divino afflante Spiritu* and of the Instruction *Sancta Mater Ecclesia* of the Biblical Commission on the historical value of the New Testament (May, 1964).[5]

A distinction has always been made between the Old and New Testaments within the Holy Scriptures. The Old Testament, in which the preparation of the coming of the Savior is recorded, is not only a propaedeutic document introducing the New Testament. By showing the roots of the Church and of Christ's doctrine in the People of the old covenant, the Hebrews and the Jews, it reveals something essential to the Christian belief in the unity of God, author of both Testaments and partner in both covenants; and it shows the profound penetration of the Church in the stuff of mankind, through the Holy People from whom she comes and through her relation with all the peoples of the earth, who are called to enter the ark of salvation and to become members of the household of God, where "there is neither Jew nor Gentile . . . but all are one in Christ Jesus".[6] In a century that has seen the worst persecution of the Jews in history—and this in a nation boasting a great Christian past—it was important that Vatican Council II insist on the perennial value of the Old Testament for the life of the faithful of Christ. This is the topic of chapter IV, in which the nature of the Old Testament, its relevance to the history of salvation, its importance for Christians, and its unity with the New Testament are briefly explained.

---

[5] The text of the instruction *Sancta Mater Ecclesia* has been published with an English translation in the *Catholic Biblical Quarterly* (July, 1964), pp. 299-312.

[6] Gal. 3, 28.

Chapter V moves to a discussion of the New Testament. It stresses the Gospels and their historical value and the influence of the early Christian community on their formation. The Acts, the Epistles and the Apocalypse are briefly described, rather too briefly in comparison with the Gospels. Why is there an imbalance in treatment between the four Gospels and the rest of the New Testament? It results less from a disregard of the Epistles than from a prevailing concern about possible inroads of Bultmann's exegetical conceptions in Catholic exegesis of the Gospels. The influence of the "post-Bultmannians" and their existential hermeneutics tends to cast doubt on the value of the four Gospels. Are these truly more than God-given occasions for existential decisions of faith? The existential exegesis of Bultmann and the "post-Bultmannians" sees no more than this in the Scriptures. Carried to its extreme, this tendency would ruin the Catholic conception of the Word of God as actually present in the reading of the Scriptures, which not only ask man questions, but also present him with God's answer as given in revelation.

At the time of the Council, such exegesis focused anxiety on the four Gospels rather than other New Testament books. For this reason chapter V appears slightly unbalanced. Yet, it was never the intention of the responsible Commission to underrate the Epistles, the Acts or the Apocalypse.

The last chapter has already been explained: it shows how Christians can and should, by assiduously reading the Scriptures of the Old and the New Testaments, increase their understanding of revelation, their fidelity to the Word of God, their communion with the three divine Persons, and, in a word, develop their spiritual life. This reading will also help to renovate theology by bringing it "back to the sources". It will renew catechetics and preaching. Bishops must promote the reading of Scripture among the people of their diocese. Priests must place their reading at the heart of their pastoral concerns.

IV

Some Theological Problems

A. *Revelation and Faith*

The approach to revelation and faith of the Constitution *Dei Filius* of Vatican Council I reflected the concerns of the second half of the 19th century: what mattered was the rationality of faith and the acceptability of revelation by reasonable beings. While the supernatural elements were not neglected, the stress lay on the compatibility of faith and reason. The Church was facing a rationalistic age and had to express her position adequately in the mentality of the time.

The situation has changed considerably since 1870. Our contemporaries are more interested in existential and personal values than in rationality. In the realm of theological research and elaboration, the climate of the 19th century, which gave apologetics a central place, is all but forgotten today. Theology is now investigating Christian experience rather than the rational aspects of revelation. It restores its mystery to revelation and its mystical dimension to assent. The steps toward faith, which used to be carefully analyzed through the evidences of credibility, rational assent, moral certitude, ecclesiastical faith and divine faith, now appear to be quite secondary. What primarily matters is the revelation itself, rather than the impact of revelation on intellectual knowledge and its importance as a source of ideas. Now we hear God speaking, revealing himself to the heart of men, whether these be the prophets, the apostles, those who, in many places and in different ways, have been selected by God to deliver his message, or even the unknown man who seeks God without knowing if he can ever find him. God revealing himself and man's personal, irreplaceable response to God are at the center of modern theological reflection on revelation.

It follows that revelation is now considered in two related dimensions. In its historical dimension, revelation has been couched in the human language of inspired authors who, in the Old or in the New Testament, have recorded the great acts of God in his dealings with men. In its personal dimension, revelation is inseparable from the act of hearing and of responding by which man acknowledges in his heart and in public that God spoke in the past and that he speaks here and now.

These aspects of the rationale of revelation are naturally emphasized in the *Constitution on Divine Revelation*. Revelation as the communication of "revealed truths" comes only at the end of the first chapter, after a condensed survey of revelation as sacred history, as *Heilsgeschichte*. Historical revelation, as recorded in the Old and New Testaments, first of all communicates realities through gestures and words, through the acted parables of the history of the Chosen People. The God who manifests himself does not speak as a professor or a scholar, but as a person. He evokes not only intellectual acceptance of what he says, but personal commitment to himself; he does not want only students and disciples, but friends attached to him through a personal relationship. This is clear in the Old Testament, where the religious attitude is essentially one of gratitude for God's loving condescension, for the lowliness of God who, without losing his transcendence, made himself friend to our Father Abraham, who spoke to Moses, who was heard by Elijah and who through all the ages speaks to the hearts of those who love him. It is still more patent in the economy of the new covenant, in the person and the life of his Son, the eternal Word made flesh for our salvation. This is the ultimate revelation that will never pass away because the Father has nothing to add once he has spoken his eternal Word and once this Word has manifested himself on earth. But the Spirit's mission is to guide men toward a loving response to Jesus the Savior. Revelation in the context of our document is the appearance of Emmanuel, of God-with-us, in the course of human history and in the texture of our lives.

The faith with which we answer this coming down of God toward us is much more than an intellectual assent. Vatican Council II on this point is neighbor to the Council of Trent and its *Decree on Justification*. Faith, for the Council of Trent, is "the beginning of human salvation, the foundation and root of all justification".[7] As Vatican Council I wrote, it is "the full assent of intellect and will to God revealing".[8] In order to be full, this assent of the will and the intellect must proceed from the whole human personality, and include, besides consent to what is said, trust in Christ, commitment, hope and love. The believer is not placed in a static situation; he is dynamically oriented toward the divine encounter in the person of Jesus

[7] *D.S.*, n. 1532.
[8] *D.S.*, n. 3008.

the Lord. His eyes are opened, and he passes from blindness to sight in an anticipation of the full vision.

The treatment of revelation by Vatican Council II is radically soteriological. That of faith is personalistic. This may become the starting point for a theology of the human person coming to spiritual maturity in his encounter with God-who-speaks.

B. *Scripture and Tradition*

The discussions on the schema *De Fontibus Revelationis* in the first session of the Council centered on one major point: Should the Church canonize the "two source" theory of revelation at a time when this theory is under revision in many theological quarters? Whereas the schema (Text I) fully endorsed the "two source" theory, a growing number of theologians had for years completely rejected this theory as inadequate and as unable to do justice to the phenomenon of Tradition and to the fullness of the presence of the Word in the written Scriptures. A short explanation of the historical aspect of this problem will lead us to the theological question itself.

The Council of Trent, as mentioned at the beginning of this introduction, said that the Gospel *i.e.,* the Good News of salvation, "is contained in written books and in unwritten traditions", and stated that it venerated them all "with an equal attitude of piety and an equal reverence". In other words, it placed on a par the Scriptures and the apostolic traditions, insofar as they convey the Gospel. In the course of the Counter-Reformation, theology was divided in the interpretation of this text. The most influential authors, following the conceptions of some pre-Tridentine theologians, interpreted this to mean that a part of the Gospel is contained in the Scriptures and another part in the apostolic traditions. The first author to state this clearly was St. Peter Canisius, whose *Catechism* became influential wherever the Counter-Reformation gained ground in German lands.[9] Meanwhile, many lesser known writers [10] continued to assume, as patristic and scholastic theology until the later Middle Ages had done, that Scripture and the apostolic traditions cannot be quantitatively divided. Far from being two sections of the deposit of revelation or, according to a formula which appeared gradually in the catechisms of the 18th and 19th centuries, two sources of faith, the Scriptures and the traditions or, equivalently, Scripture and Tradition, constitute one single whole, which is the Church's expression and handing down of the Gospel. Scripture cannot be understood apart from Tradition, for it embodies the Tradition of the apostolic Church; and its reading needs to be guided by the Holy Spirit in the Church, as manifested in the ecclesiastical documents which form the post-apostolic Tradition.

The question placed before Vatican Council II by the first form of the schema was this: Since the Council of Trent avoided the problem of the quantitative extension of Scripture and the traditions, and since Vatican Council I also shunned it, should the Council of 1962 follow these precedents or not?

---

[9] Cf. Yves Congar, *La Tradition et les Traditions,* Vol. I, Ch. 5.

[10] Cf. George Tavard, *Holy Writ or Holy Church* (New York: Harper, 1959) and "Scripture and Tradition among 17th-Century Recusants," *Theological Studies* (Sept. 1964), pp. 343-85.

The discarding of this first text of the schema in November, 1962, meant that the Council refused to be tied to the recent theory of two sources of faith. It did not imply, however, that it wished to identify itself with the opposite and older view, namely, that in a certain sense all revelation may be held to be contained in Scripture. Like the Council of Trent, it refused to pass judgment on the question of the quantitative extension of Scripture and Tradition. The question is left for theologians to discuss.

In keeping with the vote of November, 1962, the subsequent drafts of the schema and the final text as adopted on October 29 and promulgated on November 18, 1965, prescind entirely from this debated question. The necessary unity of Scripture and Tradition and their value as channels of transmission of the Gospel are stressed rather than the extension of revelation in Scripture and in Tradition.

If Vatican Council II did not wish to decide any theological controversy on the question of Tradition, it nevertheless provided indirect evidence in favor of the historians who have maintained that Trent never taught the "two source" theory.[11] For, had Trent canonized such a theory, Vatican Council II could not ignore it. Since Vatican Council II consciously kept away from the "two source" theory of Tradition, such a theology cannot belong among the questions already settled by the Church's extraordinary magisterium. One may also conclude, by a similar reasoning, that the "two source" theory has no place among the truths unquestionably taught by the ordinary magisterium. If, as has been

[11] Cf. bibliography in Gabriel Moran: *Scripture and Tradition,* pp. 89-98.

asserted,[12] the ordinary magisterium, by granting the *nihil obstat* and *imprimatur* to catechisms teaching "two sources of faith" or "two sources of revelation", had fully committed itself to such a concept of Tradition, the ecumenical Council would have been bound to recognize this conception as already included in the deposit of faith preserved and taught by the universality of the bishops. By refusing to recognize this, Vatican Council II indirectly supported the opposite contention, namely, that the ordinary magisterium has never universally taught the two sources of faith, in spite of what a number of catechisms—by no means all—may have said.

The concept of Tradition that has been endorsed by the Council is described in paragraph 8. Briefly, Tradition is identified with the permanence of the apostolic proclamation in the Church. Expressed in a special manner in the Scriptures, the apostles' preaching goes on in the Church and is destined to continue until the end of time. The apostles themselves had received it from Christ; and they handed it on to the faithful in their discourses and their letters. What was thus transmitted cannot be reduced to intellectual truths expressing doctrine; rather it implies all that contributes to the life and faith of the People of God. The idea that Tradition is essentially transmission of truth cast in the form of propositions is thereby ruled out by implication. This transmission is not only a matter of teaching, but, as our text says, of "teaching, life and worship".

Understood in this realistic way, the Church's Tradition is profoundly related to Scripture. This

---

12 Cf. George Tavard, "Scripture and Tradition: Source or Sources?", *Journal of Ecumenical Studies,* Vol. 1, n. 3, pp. 445-59.

constitutes the topic of paragraph 9, which clearly teaches what I have called "the mutual inherence" of Scripture and Tradition.[13] This means that Scripture and Tradition are implied in each other. They flow from the same unique source, namely, God speaking through Christ; and they run toward the same fulfillment, which will be the eschatological flowering of the Gospel, when God will be all in all. To Scripture, Tradition only adds—though this is of paramount importance—the experience of its transmission to and through post-apostolic times, under the guidance and illumination of the Holy Scriptures. On the basis of this radical unity of Scripture and Tradition, Vatican Council II is led to endorse the formula of the Council of Trent: "equal pious affection and reverence" *(pari pietatis affectu ac reverentia)* are due to both.

C. *Tradition and Magisterium*

One of the questions that the 19th century and the subsequent modernist crisis forced upon theology concerns the relations of the magisterium to the process of transmitting and receiving revelation. To some extent this was already raised by the Reformation, since Protestantism questioned and denied the authority of the magisterium, which was dwarfed, in its eyes, by the awesomeness of the mystery of justification by faith alone. Yet, it took time for Catholic thought to cope with this problem. No satisfactory treatment of the magisterium's relevance to Tradition and to the Church's reading of Scripture could be made, as long as ecclesiology remained in its formative stage. By a natural transi-

[13] Cf. *Holy Writ or Holy Church* (Conclusion).

tion, the Counter-Reformation turned out to be the great age of the institutional aspect of ecclesiology. The magisterium gained ground in the consideration of theologians and in the organization of the Church, as it also gained confidence in itself through its political, architectural and polemical triumphs over a slightly receding Protestant wave.

One had to wait for the second half of the 19th century, however, to collect the fruits of this development as regards the theology of Tradition. Among the dominant authors of that time who devoted their thought to this question, the main contribution comes from men of the so-called Roman School, who precisely studied the problem of the place held by the magisterium in the traditional process by which the Church hands down to successive ages what it has received from preceding generations.

Starting with Giovanni Perrone (1794-1876) and reaching its high point with Johann Baptist Franzelin (1816-1886), the Roman theology of Tradition, which was part of a wider Roman theology of the Church, was characterized by the growing importance it gave to the magisterium, especially of the Roman pontiff, in the traditioning process. The other factors of Tradition receded; they became ancillary to the discerning and deciding function of the pope and, under him, the bishops. Scripture, the Fathers and the Doctors contribute to the stream of Tradition, yet the decisive factor, which actually creates Tradition by giving it the ultimate form of doctrine, is the magisterium. Some of the theologians of Vatican Council I like Carlo Passaglia (1812-1887) and Clemens Schrader (1820-1875) understood Tradition to be, in its core, the series of documents officially approved by the Church's authority; accordingly, they saw the present authority of

Tradition as centered in the authority of the episcopal body today and singularly in the supreme authority of the Bishop of Rome. In this view, the definition of papal infallibility entailed the identity of Tradition with the decisions of the supreme magisterium.

Admittedly, the 19th-century theologians did not rule out other aspects of Tradition. Franzelin popularized the distinctions that are still familiar, even though they are no longer very meaningful, between active and passive or constitutive and interpretative traditions. All of these, however, draw their sense and their binding force from their connection with the pope's teaching authority.

The modernist crisis brought this movement to its logical extreme: for Louis Billot (1846-1936), reacting against the immanentist notion of doctrine propagated by modernism, the magisterium is the Tradition.

What took place in this progressive identification of magisterium and Tradition was primarily a narrowing down of the formerly very wide concept of Tradition to what was only one of its factors, the *regula fidei* or rule of faith, originally destined to act as the standard by which a tradition would be judged to be authentic. In the Roman theology of the 19th century, the rule of faith was simply identified with Tradition, thus impoverishing the latter considerably. For although the *regula fidei* has always been held to contain the core of faith, it was never meant to be exhaustive. The equation between rule of faith and Tradition was accompanied by a shift of meaning in the very notion of rule of faith. For the Church Fathers, who originally introduced the concept, the rule of faith is the faith accepted and taught in the past. It is known by the teaching of the main Sees and primarily by that of the Roman See. In a derivative and slightly narrower sense, it is the Creed, especially that of the Councils of Nicaea and Constantinople. In the line of thought of the 19th century, this came to mean that faith is not established by turning to the past, but by listening to the voice of the present-day magisterium, which has inherited the rule of faith and now teaches it with authority.

Paragraph 10 is the relevant passage of the *Constitution on Divine Revelation*. Here, the dual unity of Scripture and Tradition becomes a trilogy, of which the Church's magisterium constitutes the third term. However, far from being on a par with either Scripture or Tradition, the magisterium is at their service. Its function consists in "authentically interpreting" the "deposit of God's Word", which is itself made of the unity of Scripture and Tradition. It does not interpret Scripture by itself or Tradition by itself, but their co-inherence in the deposit of the Word. Thus, the magisterium's task cannot be equated with that of exegetes or that of historians of doctrine. It resides in a higher synthesis than those of biblical or of historical theology, at the level of the Symbols of faith, the Creeds and other authentic expressions of the deposit of revelation. In no sense, therefore, may the magisterium lord it over Scripture and Tradition; on the contrary, it waits upon the Word of God, to which it listens, which it keeps and which it explains.

D. *The Development of Doctrine*

Among the problems that the theology of Tradition brought on the theological scene of the 19th century was the question of the development of doctrine. The older Church had known that doctrine develops or, in other words, that Tradition is not simply a transmission of final truths and of set statements, but a self-enlarging stream of spiritual experience. The whole ground of the defense of orthodoxy against the Arians and semi-Arians after the Council of Nicaea was that the very "rule of faith" required the introduction of *omoousios* into the Creed and the corresponding development of trinitarian thought, as warrants of fidelity to scriptural revelation. The Councils of the early Church implied the legitimacy of development, since they elaborated trinitarian and christological doctrines (Nicaea to Constantinople III, 325-680), and they upheld the cult of ikons (Nicaea II, 787), and since the appearance and acceptance of patriarchates implied developments in the hierarchical structure of the Church. The constant appeal to the Tradition of the Fathers and to the rule of faith did not, therefore, exclude a search for better formulas and for a more adequate penetration into the Christian mystery. On the contrary, this very fidelity made it possible for the Church to progress in understanding and living the renovation of the paschal mystery as the life of the Holy Spirit in her.

Toward the end of the patristic period, St. Vincent of Lerins voiced the consensus of the Fathers when he described the Church's faith as uniting "universality, antiquity and unanimity", and the rule of faith as that which has been taught "everywhere, always and by all". He did not mean to endorse a static view of the Catholic faith, for he also added, in a pregnant summary of patristic thought, that the faith of the Church of Christ increases "in each man as in the whole Church, in the succession of periods and centuries, in understanding, knowledge and wisdom, although it does so according to its own nature, namely, in the same dogma, the same sense and the same doctrine".[14]

Since then, the idea that the Catholic faith unfolds itself in the course of its transmission has been inseparable from the Catholic assent to revelation. Yet, it has seldom been the object of detailed theological reflection or of official pronouncements. This is one of the underlying realities of Catholic life which are rarely analyzed because they are constantly experienced and they therefore dominate the very reflection one can make about them. But the concept of "sacred doctrine", as it was accepted by the medieval Schoolmen, entailed a development of doctrine in the Church's interpretation of Scripture: the sacred doctrine is Holy Scripture as it unfolds itself in the experience, the practice and the reflection of the Church age after age. The interpretation of Scripture does not add anything to Scripture from the outside, yet it presides over a self-development of the revealed mystery, which, after being proclaimed, is heard; after being heard, is accepted; after being accepted, becomes life in the Christian heart. In this way, the revelation, once veiled in the sacrament of Scripture, becomes life and experience in the hearts of the faithful, doctrine and teaching in the minds and mouths of doctors and bishops. It never ceases to be Good News, the announcement of salvation and the preaching of the coming of the kingdom of God; it never stops being experienced in the mystical reenactment of the Last Supper and in the faithful's participation in the mysteries of the death and the resurrection of the Lord; yet, it also becomes a body of doctrine that can be ap-

---

[14] *Commonitorium,* cf. Kirch: *Enchiridon,* nn. 815-819.

prehended by the mind in the light of the Spirit. "Depths of understanding vary according as the soul is more intimate with him," wrote Bonaventure.[15]

In the last century John Henry Newman devoted considerable attention to this question in his *Essay on the Development of Christian Doctrine* (1844), in which he concluded that a genuine development of any point of doctrine must respect the following seven principles: preservation of its type; continuity of its principle; power of assimilation; logical sequence; anticipation of its future; conservative action upon its past; chronic vigor. These are studied at length by Newman, the gist of whose ideas in this matter is that development of doctrine, without being illogical, transcends pure logic. Doctrine grows in the fashion of a living organism, which has in its self the principles of its growth, yet whose growth is nurtured by its assimilation of outside elements. A vital process then takes place, by which an interplay between the Gospel and the situation of the world to which it is preached results in new light being thrown on the Gospel, aspects of it unveiling themselves and being perceived in their integrity for the first time.

It was not until the modernist crisis, however, that the importance of doctrinal development was perceived by theologians in general. No less than eight propositions concerning the evolution of doctrine were anathematized by the decree *Lamentabili* (July 3, 1907). The encyclical *Pascendi* (Sept. 8, 1907) condemned what it called the modernist theory concerning the origin of dogma, whch distinguished between the primary or essential core of the revelation – ultimately God himself – and

15 *In Hexaëmeron*, III, 32.

secondary symbolical expressions of this core. The dogmas of the Church are, in the modernist mind, provisional canonizations of symbolic formulations, which in the course of time become obsolete and have to be replaced by other symbols.[16] The oath against Modernism (Sept. 1, 1910) also contained the following statement: "I sincerely receive the doctrine of faith which has been transmitted from the apostles to us by the orthodox Fathers always in one same sense and one same doctrine; and I therefore reject the heretical concept of the evolution of dogmas, passing from one sense to another one which differs from what the Church formerly acknowledged." [17]

The dilemma raised by Modernism found its solution, during the modernist crisis itself, in Maurice Blondel's letter on *History and Dogma* (1903),[18] in which Blondel showed the insufficiency of the contradictory positions which he termed "extrinsicism" and "historicism". Extrinsicism removes faith from the realm of history and conceives of the supernatural as having a minimal area of contact with nature. Historicism finds that history not only carries but also creates faith, which accordingly changes and varies according to the successive moods of the times. A truly Catholic theology steers its way between these unsatisfactory philosophies, thanks to a concept and practice of Tradition as that which "anticipates and illuminates the future, and is disposed to do so by the effort which it makes to remain faithful to the past".[19] Blondel concluded that such a Tradition,

---

[16] *D.S.*, n. 3483.

[17] *D.S.*, n. 3541.

[18] Maurice Blondel, *Letter on Apologetics, and History and Dogma* (New York: Holt, 1964).

[19] *Loc. cit.* p. 268.

excluding all "fixism", implies "development" as part of the Church's ongoing experience of the faith which seeks understanding.

More systematic theologians than Blondel also treated this delicate problem with great insight during the modernist controversy, especially Antoine Gardeil, in *Le Donné Révélé et la Théologie* (1909). No thorough study of the question of doctrinal evolution, however, appeared before the book of the Spanish Dominican Marín Sola: *La Evolución Homogenea del Dogma Católico* (1923). But this study was dominated by an excessively rigid Scholastic point of view, for which logical deduction is the only final tool of doctrinal evolution. Marín Sola admitted, at least in the second edition of his book (1924), an "affective way of development", which he understood to be an intuitive anticipation of what reason and logic would later deduce from the deposit of faith. Since the publication of this volume, theologians have been divided between those who recognize logical deduction as the main instrument of doctrinal evolution, and those who admit with Newman and Blondel that doctrinal development proceeds by way of a vital process of growth for which logic alone cannot account.

The controversy launched in 1946 about what was falsely called "the new theology" brought up again the question of the development of dogma. No major work on the question, however, appeared.[20] The encyclical *Humani generis* (August

[20] The most important article is Henri de Lubac, "Le problème du développement du dogme," *Recherches de Science Religieuse* (1948), pp. 130-60. Cf. Karl Rahner, "The Development of Dogma," *Theological Investigations,* Vol. 1 (Baltimore: Helicon, 1961) , pp. 39-77; Robert L. Richard, "Contribution to a Theory of Doctrinal Development," *Continuum* (1964), pp. 505-27.

12, 1950) described in these words what it considered to be an erroneous conception:

> "They" – that is, some unidentified authors – "do not consider it absurd, but altogether necessary, that theology should substitute new concepts in place of the old ones in keeping with the various philosophies which in the course of time it uses as its instruments, so that it should give human expression to divine truths in various ways which are even somewhat opposed, but still equivalent, as they say. They add that the history of dogmas consists in reporting the various forms in which revealed truth has been clothed, forms that have succeeded one another in accordance with the different teachings and opinions that have arisen over the course of the centuries."

Clearly, Pius XII feared the resurgence of a relativistic conception of religious truth which, however, need not be associated at all with a Catholic view of the development of doctrine.

Taking account of this, the *Constitution on Divine Revelation* attempts to bring together the various ways in which Catholic theology, lately and in the past, has conceived the development of doctrine; by so doing, it brings to an end the fear of development which reaction against Modernism had fostered among some. It clears of suspicion the authors who were frowned upon after the publication of *Humani generis,* although their thought was elaborated outside the modernist or antimodernist frame of reference, within which *Humani generis* was conceived.

The relevant passage of the Constitution is in

paragraph 10, where the idea of a development of Tradition is clearly expressed. Several aspects, incentives or causes of such a development are indicated. What increases is not the objective datum of revelation: the *Constitution on Divine Revelation* perfectly agrees with the statement made in the *Constitution on the Church*: "They (*i.e.*, the Roman pontiff and the bishops) do not receive a new public revelation as belonging to the divine deposit of faith" (n. 25). It is the Church's insight into the meaning of the realities and words handed on by Tradition which becomes sharper, thereby enlarging her vision. This progress follows the converging, yet in themselves distinct, ways of contemplative study and of spiritual experience. The former pertains more to the intellectual order; the latter to that of a sense of God beyond and above the intellect. The former opens the door to man's activities at the service of a faith which seeks to understand; the latter is lived in man's passivities under the delicate brush of God's hand in the soul. The former is cataphatic; the latter, apophatic.

These ways of unfolding the mysteries of God orient the Church toward the fullness of saving truth, to which the Spirit guides her. Their final fruition will come in the eschatological encounter between the Church and her Lord, at "the ultimate fulfillment of God's words in herself" (n. 8).

E. *Hermeneutical Problems*

It is not possible in this short introduction to raise all the exegetical questions connected with chapters III, IV and V of the Constitution.

Evidently, these chapters ought to be read together with Pius XII's encyclical *Divino afflante Spiritu* (1943) and with the instruction *Sancta Mater Ecclesia* published by the Biblical Commission on August 21, 1964. The purpose of *Divino afflante Spiritu* was to endorse the renewal of biblical studies which was heralded by M. J. Lagrange in the first decades of this century and which has flourished, since then, in the works of many scholars inspired by the two great centers of Catholic exegesis, the Ecole Biblique de Jérusalem and the *Institutum Biblicum* in Rome. The purpose of the Instruction, prompted partly by recent discussions of the historical life of Jesus, partly by the debates around the Council concerning the interpretation of the New Testament, was to set down norms for the study of the historical character of the four Gospels. It was important to place at the Council fathers' disposal an authoritative compendium of recent research relative to the criticism of the New Testament, as this has been found acceptable to Catholic exegesis. Brief comments on a few points pertinent to exegesis will be appropriate.

The Canon of the Bible

The Constitution provides no list of the canonical books, the decrees of the Councils of Florence (*Bulla unionis Coptorum*, commonly called *Decretum pro Jacobitis*, February 2, 1442, *C.O.D.*, p.548; *D.S.*, n.1334-1335) and of Trent (Session IV, April 8, 1546; *C.O.D.*, pp.639-40; *D.S.*, n. 1502-1503) being sufficiently clear. The Catholic Church admits as equally inspired and canonical both the protocanonical books of the Hebrew Bible of Jerusalem and the deuterocanonical books – usually named "apocrypha" by Protestant authors –

contained in the Greek Bible of Alexandria called the *Septuagint.* These are usually not admitted by Protestants, although they were ordinarily printed as an appendix to the Old Testament until the British and Foreign Bible Society decided to do away with this practice in 1826.[21]

Texts and Translations

The Council specifically mentions the Greek *Septuagint* as traditional since the beginning of the Church. Already quoted in the New Testament, this version deserves a privileged place on a par with the available Hebrew texts. The Latin *Vulgate* and other Latin versions, as well as the "other Oriental translations", are said to have "always been honored" in the Church. Other translations, well adapted to the many modern vernaculars, are recommended in general: they should be made mainly on the original texts, and, at the opportune time, in common with scholars of other Churches. This passage, which happily completes the corresponding text of the Council of Trent,[22] should do away with the mistaken, yet still widely spread, notion that the Latin *Vulgate* contains the only official text of the Bible.

Inspiration

As explained in the *Constitution on Divine Revelation* (n.11), the doctrine of scriptural inspiration holds God to be the author of the books of the Bible: this fact provides the basis for their canonicity, which is simply the Church's recogni-

---

[21] S. L. Greenslade, ed., *The Cambridge History of the Bible* (1963), p. 391.

[22] *D.S.*, n. 1508.

tion of their divine authorship. Yet, the human writers and redactors are also "truly authors", in the ordinary sense of human authorship, of their books. The relations between these two simultaneous authorships are not investigated here, as they belong to a field where several theories may be proposed and debated without threat to the basic doctrine. At any rate, God expressed himself through the literary qualities and methods of men whom he guided through the charism of inspiration which is described in the encyclicals *Providentissimus Deus* of Leo XIII (Nov. 18, 1893; *D.S.,* n.3291-3294) and *Divino afflante Spiritu* of Pius XII.[23]

Inerrancy is a consequence of, yet cannot be equated with, inspiration. Whereas inspiration implies an active or positive guidance of the human author's mind by the Holy Spirit, inerrancy is simply a preservation from error, which is more passive and negative. The salient fact in this matter is that the Constitution avoids the term "inerrancy" on account of its negative tonality. Instead of presenting Scripture in the negative perspective of its freedom from error, it prefers to stress positively its teaching of the truth "firmly, faithfully and without error". The truth in question is that "which God decided to put down in the sacred writings for our salvation's sake" (n.11). Attention to the problem of inerrancy is thus oriented in two directions. In the first place, Holy Scripture is free from errors as regards the truth of salvation, but not necessarily in merely philosophical or scientific matters. In the second, God's positive guidance of

---

[23] Cf. Pierre Benoît, "Révélation et inspiration selon la Bible, chez saint Thomas et dans les discussions modernes," *Revue Biblique* (1963), pp. 321-70.

the author into the truth is more important than its negative consequence of inerrancy, and should become the focus of theological reflection on inspiration.

Interpretation

Scriptural interpretation, or hermeneutics, is approached in a broad way, for the Council need obviously not lay out detailed regulations, or restrict legitimate freedom of research within the framework of Catholic Tradition. The instructions already published by Pius XII and by the Biblical Commission are in no way superseded by the *Constitution on Divine Revelation;* rather, they are solemnly endorsed for the encouragement of Catholic exegetes and the further development of biblical studies both at the scholarly and at the more popular levels.

Especially pertinent to the interpretation of the Bible are the following points:

(a) The Old and the New Testaments belong together. The Church cannot forget or forgo her roots in the People of God from whom the Savior came. The Old Testament, recording the main stages of the preparation of mankind for Christ's advent, is truly the Word of God, just like the New, which reports the fulfillment of salvation-history in Christ and in the apostolic community centered on the faith in his resurrection. They both formulate and foster man's response to God in living and loving faith. Therefore, one should read the Old and the New together for the light which each throws upon the other.

(b) Both Testaments are at the same time historical records of the events of salvation and profoundly spiritual writings in which the Word speaks to man in the Spirit. For this reason the Church maintains that they are sufficiently accurate, as concerns sacred history, and that they are also open to a spiritual understanding reaching beyond the documentary letter to the supernatural depth of what history reports.

(c) In order to assess the historical sense, one should study the literary forms of the various biblical books (n.12), as *Divino afflante Spiritu* clearly indicated and as exegetes have done for a long time. The genre of the New Testament and especially of the four Gospels implies the true history of what Christ said and did (n.19), even though, as the instruction *Sancta Mater Ecclesia* explained, this history took the kerygmatic form of a living testimony for the ultimate purpose of preaching and spreading the Good News.

(d) Catholic Tradition has always paid great attention to the spiritual sense, or senses, of the text, concerning the history of which major works have been published by Father Henri de Lubac.[24] Primarily, this means that biblical interpretation goes further than the discovery of the literal or historical sense reached by scientific exegesis. It also tries to discern the sense intended by the Spirit, not only for the original readers or hearers of the Word, but for those who at all times and in all places will be eager to hear the Word in their reading of the Scriptures and to keep it. Commonly called "spiritual" in the past, and traditionally divided into three senses (allegorical, tropological, anagogical), this dimension of Scripture underwent a partial eclipse during the 18th and 19th centuries.

---

[24] *Histoire et Esprit: l'intelligence de l'Ecriture d'après Origène, 1950; Exégèse Mediévale: les quatre sens de l'Ecriture,* 4 Vols., 1959-1964.

It has reappeared in our times under the influence of historical studies of patristic and medieval exegesis and under the impact of biblical theology, which opened insights into the typology of the Bible[25] (typological sense) and into its *sensus plenior* or fuller sense.[26] Without entering current discussions, in which it does not want to take sides, the Council gives the green light to continued studies along these lines, by insisting on the role of the analogy of faith in interpreting Scripture (n.12), on the unity of the two Testaments (n.16), on the everlasting worth of Scripture as, "for the Church, support and vigor, for the Church's children, strength of the faith, food of the soul, source of the spiritual life" (n.21), on searching for "a day by day deeper understanding" (n.23), on the place of Scripture as "the soul of sacred theology" (n.24), on interiorly listening to the Word (n.25), on Scripture reading as the initiation of a "dialogue between God and man" (n.25).

F. *A Theology of the Word*

The Constitution reaches its highest point in the last chapter: "Holy Scripture in the Church's Life." Shortly before the opening of the 3rd session, Pope Paul VI, in a radio speech to the 80th *Katholikentag* meeting at Stuttgart, said: "The Word of God is a light that gives strength and consolation to our life. The Word of God, which, for the Council fathers, constitutes the supreme authority and the symbolic center, is also the soul

---

[25] Cf. Jean Daniélou, *From Shadows to Reality* (Westminster, Md.: Newman, 1960).

[26] Cf. Raymond E. Brown, *The Sensus Plenior of the Sacred Scripture*, 1955.

of your deliberations."[27] In these few words, Paul VI expressed his interest in what should be the ultimate fruit of the *Constitution on Divine Revelation,* namely, that the Word of God may become the heart of both doctrine and life in the Church. In order to grasp this potential value of the Constitution, one ought to remember that, during the preparatory phase of the Council, the Secretariat for Promoting Christian Unity had written a project for a constitution or decree on "the Word of God". This project was never formally presented to the Council for discussion, although the Archbishop of Durban (South Africa), Denis Hurley, in his conciliar speech of November 19, 1962, asked for an immediate debate on "the excellent schema *De Verbo Dei*". However, the reporter of this chapter in the Council, the Bishop of Haarlem (Holland), Johannes van Dodewaard, noted in his report that the last chapter of the Constitution had been composed with the help of the schema *De Verbo Dei* prepared by the Secretariat for Promoting Christian Unity.

This last chapter should be read, not only as a fitting conclusion for the *Constitution on Divine Revelation,* but also as a starting point for an opening of the Catholic concern for Scripture, for Tradition and for a pastoral reading and preaching of Scripture, to a broader interest in a theology of the Word. Since the 16th century, Catholicism in general has shied away from placing the Word at the center of its theology, mainly through a fear of Protestant interpretations of the centrality of the Word in doctrine and preaching. Although the great Catholic preachers of the 17th century,

---

[27] *Documentation Catholique* (Oct. 4, 1963), n. 1433, col. 1230.

Bossuet, Mabillon, Massillon and their lesser colleagues, understood their function as "sacred orators" to be that of instruments of God's Word, the theological synthesis of the Counter-Reformation, by and large, included no like insight. In the course of time, knowledge of the text of the Bible by both clergy and laity waned. Fewer and fewer priests preached on biblical themes, and fewer and fewer laymen used the Bible for the daily food and expression of their piety. Of late, however, a reaction has started, and reflections on the Word of God have become more frequent in theological literature.

The ultimate purpose of the *Constitution on Divine Revelation* is to invite all Catholics to restore the written and preached Word to its centrality in theology and in worship. The Constitution insists that, in the Scriptures, God the Father himself addresses his children so that the very strength and vigor of the Church comes from his Word. There must follow a diligent scanning of Scripture by those who enjoy gifts of scholarship. Their purpose should not be to satisfy intellectual curiosity, but to enrich spiritual life and theology. For theological reflection cannot be severed from the live font of divine wisdom in which God speaks to us. "The study of the sacred page" should be "like the soul of sacred theology" (n.24). By the same token, it should be the soul of preaching and catechesis, so that it may eventually become the daily food of the faithful.

Both clergy and laity are encouraged to read Scripture. Yet, reading will not help much unless it contributes to transform our mind in the light of biblical thought. Since the Scriptures constitute the very form of revelation and embody the human language in which God couched his self-manifestation to men, the mentality of the biblical authors and the characteristics of the Semitic way of thinking and praying should be felt throughout the Christian approach to worship, to faith and to the application of faith to world problems. A theology of the Word should start here. It could solve the pastoral problems formerly raised by the advocates of "kerygmatic theology", and it would help Catholic thought to unloose its ties to Western culture and civilization, thereby making itself more ready to encounter world cultures and world religions. The biblical forms of thought came from a Semitic, near-Eastern environment, at the crossroad of the great civilizations of Europe in the West, of Asia in the East and of Africa in the South and Southwest. The historical circumstances, which directed the spread of Christianity to the West by way of the Roman Empire and of Hellenistic culture, have now run their appointed course. The time has come for a re-orientation of Christian ways of thought and forms of worship toward the other corners of the earth. This has already been anticipated by the geographic spread of revelation over all continents. Nevertheless, the missionary expansion of the Church cannot bear its fruits as long as it is not accompanied by a translation of Christian revelation in the categories of non-Western minds.

By helping us to rediscover the Gospel in its pristine form, a theology of the Word will be the means by which the Church's Tradition will expand beyond the limits of the Greco-Roman world. In this way alone can we become fully Catholic.

V

The Constitution on Divine Revelation in the Council's Work

None of the documents adopted by Vatican Council II should be read in isolation from the others. Granted that each one has its own meaning in itself, which is to be determined by its structure and by the theological context of the problem it deals with, this meaning receives new light from the general renovation of the Church undertaken by the Council as a whole. The *Constitution on Divine Revelation* should therefore be read in conjunction with the other documents of the Council, especially with the *Constitution on the Church,* the *Constitution on the Sacred Liturgy* and the *Decree on Ecumenism.*

In particular, the following points should be noticed. The prologue and the first chapter of the *Constitution on the Sacred Liturgy* explain the principles of a theology of the Word in the framework of the liturgical action. The liturgical Constitution as a whole is strongly biblical in tone, and it invites all the faithful to renovate their liturgical spirit along the lines of a biblical theology of the Word. Readers of the *Constitution on Divine Revelation* should compare its last chapter with the *Constitution on the Sacred Liturgy,* nn. 7 (on the presence of the Word who speaks when the Scriptures are read in the liturgical assembly), 24, 33, 35, 51, 52 (where principles of liturgical participation in regard to the scriptural readings are explained, and practical norms of liturgical reforms determined).

Along similar lines, the Council emphasizes the importance and value of Scripture reading for priests (*The Ministry and Life of Priests,* nn. 5, 15), who are also, together with the bishops, ministers of the Word (nn. 2, 8), for religious (*The Adaptation and Renewal of Religious Life,* n. 6), and for seminarians (*Priestly Training,* n. 16).

The chapters on the "Mystery of the Church" and on the "People of God" in the *Constitution on the Church* are also profoundly scriptural, and their ecclesiology is essentially biblical. On some specific points the *Constitution on the Church* and the *Constitution on Divine Revelation* throw light on each other. Paragraph 12 in the *Constitution on the Church,* which explains the "sense of faith" and the charisms of the Christian people, is relevant to a theology of the development of doctrine (*Constitution on Divine Revelation,* n. 8). This same problem of doctrinal development may be fruitfully illustrated by paragraph 25 in the *Constitution on the Church,* on the infallibility of the Roman pontiff: this text contains an interpretation of the definition of Vatican Council I, to which it adds the significant complement that, while pontifical definitions are infallible in themselves (*ex sese*), and not on account of consent of the Church (*non autem ex consensus Ecclesiae),* the Church's assent, however, can never be missing (*assensus Ecclesiae numquam deesse potest*). The concept of the Church's collegiality, in which this precision is grounded, itself provides a good example of a doctrinal development in ecclesiology.

Chapter VII (*Constitution on the Church*), on the eschatological vocation of Christians, should be read in the perspective of the last chapter of the *Constitution on Divine Revelation*: a pastoral reevaluation of Scripture-reading is bound to make the faithful much more aware of their heavenly citizenship and of their transitory status and pilgrim state in this world.

The last chapter (*Constitution on the Church*), on the Virgin Mary, Forth-bringer of God (*Deipara, Theotokos*), vividly illustrates what the *Constitution on Divine Revelation* (nn. 7-10) says on the relationships of Scripture and Tradition: the scriptural testimony concerning the Virgin is to be read in the context of the Church's living Tradition, for the Holy Spirit is always at work, bringing us the understanding of all that Christ has said.

VI

Ecumenical Importance of the Constitution

The relevance of the *Decree on Ecumenism* for the theology of revelation comes mainly from the fact that in ecumenical circles outside of Catholicism the question of Scripture and Tradition has also been intensely studied in the past few years. In the World Council of Churches, the Faith and Order Assembly of Montreal (July, 1963) brought to its completion the work of two commissions on Tradition, and published an important document on this topic, in the elaboration of which Orthodox and Protestants collaborated. In the United States, the Consultation for Church Union, at its meeting at Oberlin, Ohio (April, 1962), adopted a very remarkable report on "Scripture, Tradition and the Guardians of Tradition".

Owing to the importance of this question in Catholic-Protestant conversations, the Council's *Decree on Ecumenism* devoted the following passage to it:

A love and reverence—almost a cult—of Holy Scripture leads our brethren to a constant and diligent study of the sacred text. For the Gospel "is the power of God for salvation to everyone who has faith, to the Jew first and then to the Greek" (Rom. 1, 16).

While invoking the Holy Spirit, they seek in these very Scriptures God as he speaks to them in Christ, the one whom the prophets foretold, the Word of God made flesh for us. In the Scriptures they contemplate the life of Christ, as well as the teachings and the actions of the divine master for the salvation of men, in particular the mysteries of his death and resurrection.

But when Christians separated from us affirm the divine authority of the Sacred Books, they think differently from us—different ones in different ways—about the relationship between the Scriptures and the Church. For in the Church, according to Catholic belief, its authentic teaching office has a special place in expounding and preaching the written Word of God.

Nevertheless, in the dialogue itself, the sacred Word is a precious instrument in the mighty hand of God for attaining to that unity which the Savior holds out to all men (n. 21).

Since the entire Christian world is now re-examining its varying concepts and practices of Tradition, the Council's refusal to endorse the "two source" theory of revelation constitutes a prominent milestone in the development of Catholic-Protestant conversations and a great step forward toward an ecumenical consensus. The continuing dialogue which is advocated by the *Decree on Ecumenism* should find great encouragement in the *Constitution on Divine Revelation.*

De Divina Revelatione

THE

DOGMATIC CONSTITUTION

ON

DIVINE REVELATION

OF

VATICAN COUNCIL II

Promulgated by Pope Paul VI
November 18, 1965

Some minor points should be noted concerning the following translation.

The references given in the text and all but one of the footnotes belong to the Constitution itself. The reader will notice that some of the biblical references specify that the Greek text of the New Testament is being quoted or alluded to. In all other instances, the reference is to the Latin Vulgate.

I have found it necessary to add a footnote of my own, the first in Chapter 3. This is numbered 16a in order not to break the sequence of the Constitution's official footnotes. This footnote is self-explanatory.

All the official footnotes refer to biblical passages or ecclesiastical documents. In some cases they mention one or two recent editions where one may read the passage in question: I have put these between parentheses. References to Denzinger's *Enchiridion Symbolorum* contain two numbers: the first is that of the old edition, Denzinger-Bannwart; the second is that of the newer edition, Denzinger-Schönmetzer.

The few lines following the last chapter do not belong to the Constitution as such. They constitute the formula of promulgation. Although, for brevity's sake, Pope Paul's name alone follows, the Constitution was promulgated by the entire Council, that is, by Pope Paul together with the Council fathers.

GEORGE H. TAVARD

PAUL BISHOP

SERVANT OF THE SERVANTS OF GOD

TOGETHER WITH THE FATHERS OF THE SACRED COUNCIL

COMMITS TO PERMANENT RECORD

THE DOGMATIC CONSTITUTION ON DIVINE REVELATION

PROLOGUE

TO THE WORD OF GOD this holy Synod listens carefully. It proclaims it fearlessly and makes these words of St. John its own: "We announce to you the eternal life, which was with the Father and has appeared to us. We announce to you what we have seen and heard, that you may commune with us and that our communion be with the Father and with his Son, Jesus Christ" (1 John 1, 2-3). Following the Council of Trent and the first Council of the Vatican, it intends to explain the authentic doctrine concerning divine revelation and its transmission, so that the whole world, hearing, may trust the message of salvation—trusting, may hope—hoping, may love.[1]

---

[1] Cf. St. Augustine, *De catechizandis rudibus,* ch. IV, n. 8 (*P.L.*, p. 40, 316).

CHAPTER I

Revelation

2. It has pleased God in his goodness and wisdom to reveal himself, and to make known the secret hidden in his will (cf. Eph. 1, 9): through Christ, the Word made flesh, and in the Holy Spirit, men have access to the Father and are made sharers in the divine nature (cf. Eph. 2, 18; 2 Pet. 1, 4). In this revelation the invisible God (cf. Col. 1, 15; 1 Tim. 1, 17), prompted by his overflowing love, addresses men as friends (cf. Ex. 33, 11; John 15, 14-15) and converses with them, (cf. Bar. 3, 38) with the purpose of inviting and receiving them into communion with himself. This revelation is effected in interrelated actions and words: the works performed by God in the history of salvation point up and confirm the doctrine and the realities expressed by his words; the words proclaim his works and throw light on the mystery contained in them. Through this revelation the profound truth concerning God and human salvation shines for us in Christ, who is at the same time the mediator and the fullness of the whole revelation.[2]

3. God, who creates and preserves all through his Word (cf. John 1, 3), presents men with a

---

[2] Cf. Matt. 11, 27; John 1, 14 and 17; 14, 6; 17, 1-3; 2 Cor. 3, 16 and 4, 6; Eph. 1, 3-14.

perennial testimony to himself in created things. With the purpose of opening the way of salvation from heaven (cf. Rom. 1, 19-20), he furthermore manifested himself to our first parents in the beginning. After their fall, he raised them, by a promise of redemption, to hope in salvation (cf. Gen. 3, 15); and he watched over mankind without failing, ready to give eternal life to all those who seek salvation by persistent well-doing (cf. Rom. 2, 6-7). At his own good time he called Abraham to make him into a great nation (cf. Gen. 12, 2); after the patriarchs, he taught the nation, through Moses and the prophets, to acknowledge him as the only living and true God, the prudent Father and the just Judge, and to expect the promised Savior. Through the centuries, he thus prepared the way for the Gospel.

4. After speaking many times in many ways in the prophets, God "finally, in these very days, has spoken to us in the Son" (Heb. 1, 1-2). He sent his Son, the eternal Word who enlightens all men, to dwell among men and tell them the secrets of God (cf. John 1, 1-18). Jesus Christ, therefore, the Word made flesh, "a man sent to men",[3] "speaks God's words" (John 3, 34) and fulfills the saving task entrusted to him by the Father (cf. John 5, 36; 17, 4). To see him is to see the Father (cf. John 14, 9). Thus, by all his presence and self-manifestation, by his words and his works, by his symbolic actions and his miracles, especially by his death and his glorious resurrection from the dead, he—the Spirit of truth being finally sent—brings revelation to perfection by fulfilling it, and confirms it with the divine witness: God is among us to free us from

[3] *Epistola ad Diognetum,* ch. VII, n. 4 (Funk: *Patres Apostolici,* I, p. 403).

the darkness of sin and death, and to raise us up into eternal life.

The Christian order, which is the new and final covenant, shall never pass away. No further public revelation is to be expected until the glorious manifestation of our Lord Jesus Christ (cf. 1 Tim. 6, 14; Tit. 2, 13).

5. To God who reveals himself is due the "obedience of faith" (Rom. 16, 26; cf. Rom. 1, 5; 2 Cor. 10, 5-6), by which man freely pledges himself to God, giving "God the full submission of his intelligence and will" [4] and voluntarily assenting to the revelation he has made. For such a faith to be born, man needs to be prepared and assisted by God's grace and the interior helps of the Holy Spirit, who will move and turn the heart to God, open the eyes of the mind and give "all men joy in consenting to and believing the truth".[5] Unceasingly, the same Holy Spirit so perfects faith through his gifts that the understanding of revelation may become more profound.

6. In divine revelation God has wanted to show and to share himself and the eternal decisions of his will concerning men's salvation, "that they may participate in the divine wealth, which utterly exceeds the human mind's comprehension".[6]

This holy Synod recognizes that "God, the beginning and the end of all things, may be known with certainty by the natural light of human reason reflecting on created things" (cf. Rom. 1, 20). It

---

[4] Vatican Council I, *Constitutio dogmatica de fide catholica,* ch. 3 (*Denz.* 1789; 3008).

[5] 2nd Council of Orange, canon 7 (*Denz.* 180; 377); Vatican Council I, *loc. cit.* (*Denz.* 1791; 3010).

[6] Vatican Council I, *Constitutio dogmatica de fide catholica,* ch. 2 (*Denz.* 1786; 3005).

teaches, however, that it is due to revelation that "in the present condition of mankind, the divine realities, which are not in themselves beyond the reach of human reason, may be known by all in a short time, with firm certainty and without error".[7]

[7] *Ibid.* (*Denz.* 1785 and 1786; 3004 and 3005).

Study-Club Questions

1. The *Constitution on Divine Revelation* establishes a new milestone along the way pointed out by the Council of Trent and Vatican Council I concerning the nature of revelation and man's means of perceiving it. (a) What was Trent's attitude toward the relationship between Scripture and Tradition? (b) What was Vatican Council I's attitude? (c) How did they complement each other?
2. God's revelation of himself is effected in interrelated actions and words. What are these interrelated actions and words?
3. Briefly discuss how, through the centuries, God prepared the way for the Gospel.
4. Why is revelation (a) neither essentially a doctrine, (b) nor a set of propositions and formulations to be believed, (c) nor the promulgation of an ethical law of prescription and proscription?
5. The purpose of this conciliar Constitution is to be assessed, as its history clearly shows, less in the light of the polemical implications of the text originally prepared, than in the perspective in which the successive revisions were made, guided as they were by the conciliar debates and by the instructions given by Pope John to the mixed Commission that he created. Explain.
6. Revelation is now considered in two related dimensions: (a) historical, (b) personal. Briefly discuss this dual relationship.
7. How does the first and last chapter of the Constitu-

tion constitute the general framework of the document and of the doctrine it teaches?

8. How did Christ bring revelation to perfection? Why can there be no more public revelation? Can there be any private revelation?
9. How is man able to believe in God's revelation? How does the Holy Spirit help man to believe?
10. How can God be known with certainty by the natural light of human reason reflecting on created things?
11. How can we be sure that due to revelation divine realities may be known by all (a) in a short time, (b) with firm certainty, (c) and without error?
12. The treatment of Revelation by Vatican Council II is radically soteriological; that of faith is personalistic. What far-reaching theological effects does this statement imply—if any?
13. Why do you think Vatican Council II refused to pass judgment on the question of the quantitative extension of Scripture and Tradition?
14. What did the Church Fathers—who originally introduced the term—mean by "the rule of faith"?
15. Briefly discusss the idea of "mutual inherence" of Scripture and Tradition.

CHAPTER II

The Transmission of Divine Revelation

7. God mercifully provided that what he had revealed for the salvation of all nations should be integrally preserved forever and transmitted to all generations. For this purpose, Christ the Lord, in whom the entire revelation of God Most High is brought to completion (cf. 2 Cor. 1, 20; 3, 16–4, 6), commissioned the apostles to preach the Gospel to all—formerly promised through the prophets, and now fulfilled and orally proclaimed by himself—as the source of all saving truth and moral discipline: thus they would bestow God's gifts on men.[8] This was faithfully done by the apostles: in what they preached, did and instituted, they handed on what they had received from Christ, in his words, his way of life and his works, or what they had learned at the Holy Spirit's suggestions. This was also done by the apostles and the apostolic men who, inspired by the same Holy Spirit, wrote down the news of salvation.[9]

---

[8] Cf. Matt. 28, 19-20; Mark 16, 15; Council of Trent, session IV, Decree *De Canonicis Scripturis* (*Denz.* 783; 1501).

[9] Cf. Council of Trent, *loc. cit.;* Vatican Council I, session III, *Constitutio dogmatica de fide catholica,* ch. 2 (*Denz.* 1787; 3006).

That the Gospel might be kept integral and alive without interruption in the Church, the apostles gave themselves successors, the bishops, to whom they handed on "their own teaching responsibility".[10] This holy transmission and the Holy Scripture of the two covenants are therefore like a looking glass in which the pilgrim Church on earth contemplates God, from whom she receives all, until the time when she will be led to see him face to face as he is (cf. 1 John 3, 2).

8. Thus, the apostolic preaching, which is expressed in a unique way in the inspired books, had to be kept continually until the end of time. Whence, handing on what they themselves received, the apostles exhort the faithful to maintain the traditions they have learned, whether by word of mouth or by mail (cf. 2 Thess. 2, 15), and to fight for the faith once received (cf. Jude 3).[11] What has been transmitted by the apostles contains all that leads to the sanctification of the life of the People of God and to the growth of faith. Likewise the Church, in her doctrine, life and worship, perpetuates and transmits to all generations all that she is and all that she believes.

The Tradition that issues from the apostles progresses in the Church under the assistance of the Holy Spirit.[12] Insight into the realities and the words transmitted grows: this results from contemplation and study by the faithful who ponder over them in their heart (cf. Luke 2, 19 and 51),

---

10 St. Irenaeus, *Adversus Haereses,* III, 3, 1 (*P.G.* 7, 848; Harvey, 2, p. 9).

11 Cf. 2nd Council of Nicaea (*Denz.* 303; 602); 4th Council of Constantinople, session X, canon 1 (*Denz.* 336; 650-652).

12 Cf. Vatican Council I, *Constitutio dogmatica de fide catholica,* ch. 4: *de fide et ratione* (*Denz.* 1800; 3020).

from their experience of a profound understanding of spiritual realities, from the preaching of those who, with the episcopal succession, received the unfailing charism of the truth. Through the centuries the Church always strives after the fullness of divine truth, until the ultimate fulfillment of God's words in herself.

The sayings of the holy Fathers witness to the life-giving presence of this Tradition, whose riches are poured into the experience and life of the believing and praying Church. Through the same Tradition, the integral list of the sacred books becomes known to the Church, and the sacred letters themselves are understood in their depths and made indefectibly contemporary in her. In this way, God, who spoke in the past, unceasingly talks to the bride of his beloved Son; and the Holy Spirit—through whom the living voice of the Gospel is raised in the Church and, through her, in the world—leads believers into all truth and makes the Word of Christ dwell in them abundantly (cf. Col. 3, 16).

9. Holy Tradition, then, and Holy Scripture are closely interconnected and they intercommunicate. For, flowing from the same divine source, they both somehow join into one and run toward the same end. Holy Scripture is God's own speech as written under the influx of the divine Spirit; by holy Tradition, God's Word, entrusted to the apostles by the Lord Christ and the Holy Spirit, is relayed integrally to their successors, so that, following the light of the Spirit of truth, these may faithfully preserve, expound and spread it in their discourses. Consequently, the Church does not draw her certainty about all that is revealed with the help of Holy Scripture alone. Both are, therefore,

to be received and venerated with equal pious affection and reverence.[13]

10. Holy Tradition and Holy Scripture form the one sacred deposit of God's Word which has been entrusted to the Church. By adhering to it, all the holy People, together with its pastors, perseveres in the apostles' doctrine and communion, in the breaking of the bread and in prayer (cf. Acts 2, 42, Greek text). Thus, the remarkable harmony of bishops and faithful comes into being in the preservation, the practice and the confession of the traditional faith.[14]

The task of providing an authentic interpretation of God's Word in Scripture or Tradition [15] has been entrusted only to the Church's living magisterium,[16] whose authority is wielded in the name of Jesus Christ. This magisterium is not above God's Word; it rather serves the Word, teaching only what has been transmitted, as, by divine mandate and with the Holy Spirit's assistance, it listens to God's Word with piety, keeps it in awe and expounds it with fidelity. All that it puts forward to be believed as divinely revealed, it draws from this one deposit of faith. Patently, therefore, Holy Tradition, Holy Scripture and the Church's magisterium are,

---

13 Cf. Council of Trent, session IV, *loc. cit.* (*Denz.* 783; 1501).

14 Cf. Pius XII: Apostolic Constitution *Munificentissimus Deus,* Nov. 1, 1950 (*Acta Apostolicae Sedis* 42 [1950], p. 756), with reference to the words of St. Cyprian, *Epistola 66,* 8 (Hartel, III, B, p. 733): "The Church, the people united to its Priest and the flock following its Shepherd . . ."

15 Cf. Vatican Council I, *Constitutio de fide catholica,* ch. 3 (*Denz.,* 1792, 3011).

16 Cf. Pius XII: Encyclical Letter *Humani generis,* Aug. 12, 1950 (*A.A.S.* 42 [1950], pp. 568-9; *Denz.* 2314; 3886).

according to God's wise design, so interconnected and united that none can stand without the others, and that all together effectively contribute, each in its own way, under the motion of the one Holy Spirit, to the salvation of souls.

Study-Club Questions

1. How did the apostles—in what they preached, did and instituted—proclaim the Gospel to all men?
2. What has been transmitted by the apostles contains all that leads to sanctification of the life of the People of God and to the growth of faith. Discuss.
3. How does the Tradition that issues from the apostles advance in the Church under the assistance of the Holy Spirit?
4. Scripture and Tradition form the one deposit of God's Word which has been entrusted to the Church. (a) How does Scripture relay God's Word? (b) How does Tradition relay God's Word?
5. Briefly discuss the interconnection and unity of (a) Scripture, (b) Tradition, (c) and the Church's magisterium.
6. What is the concept of Tradition that has been endorsed by Vatican Council II?
7. In the Roman theology of the 19th century, the rule of faith was simply identified with Tradition, thus impoverishing the latter considerably. Briefly discuss the effects of this progressive identification of magisterium and Tradition.
8. Mention some examples of how historical revelation, as recorded in the Old and New Testaments, communicates realities through (a) gestures and words, (b) through the acted parables of the history of the Chosen People?
9. The faith with which we answer this coming down

of God toward man is much more than an intellectual assent. Why?

10. Can Scripture and Tradition be quantitatively divided?
11. What is the difference between the Church's extraordinary magisterium and ordinary magisterium?
12. Mention some of the ways in which the magisterium interprets the "deposit of God's Word".
13. Tradition is not simply a transmission of final truths and of set statements, but a self-enlarging stream of spiritual experience. Explain.
14. The interpretation of Scripture does not add anything to Scripture from the outside; yet it presides over a self-development of the revealed mystery, which, after being proclaimed, is heard; after being heard, is accepted; after being accepted, becomes life in the Christian heart. Mention some examples of doctrinal development in the Church.
15. How important is John Henry Newman's conclusion that a genuine development of any point of doctrine must respect the following seven principles: (a) preservation of its type; (b) continuity of its principle; (c) power of assimilation; (d) logical sequence; (e) anticipation of its future; (f) conservative action upon its past; (g) chronic vigor?

CHAPTER III
Holy Scripture: Divine Inspiration and Interpretation

11. Divine revelation, which is contained and presented in Holy Scripture, was committed to writing under the Holy Spirit's influx.[16a] Following the

---

[16a] As published by the *Osservatore Romano* (Nov. 19, 1965), the Latin text of the Constitution contains this sentence in the following form: *"Divinitus revelata, quae in Sacra Scriptura litteris continentur et prostant, Spiritu Sancto afflante consignata sunt."* This was already the version voted on on October 19, 1965. However, the location of the word *litteris* here results from an editor's or a printer's error. This can be easily seen: whereas the above form of the sentence appears for the first time in the booklet presenting the amendments to the Council Fathers (*Schema Constitutionis Dogmaticae De Divina Revelatione: Modi a Patribus Conciliaribus propositi a Commissione Doctrinali examinati,* p. 40), the same booklet contains the sentence in another form on p. 32, where the meaning of the amendment is explained: *"Divinitus revelata, quae in Sacra Scriptura continentur et prostant, Spiritu Sancto afflante litteris consignata sunt."* The explanation given at this point, which makes sense in relation to *this* form of the sentence, cannot correspond to the form it has on p. 40. That *litteris* goes with *consignata* rather than with *continentur* seems also clear from a grammatical point of view. The previous schemas followed the pattern of p. 32, which therefore belongs to the text as endorsed by the Council in September 1965. It is this version which our translation follows.

apostolic faith, our holy Mother the Church holds the complete books of the Old and the New Testaments, with all their parts, to be sacred and canonical. For, written under the Holy Spirit's inspiration (cf. John 20, 31; 2 Tim. 3, 16; 2 Pet. 1, 19-21; 3, 15-16), they are authored by God and have been handed on to the Church as such.[17] To compose the sacred books, God selected men whom he assisted in the use of their faculties and talents; [18] since he acted in and through them,[19] they, as genuine authors, would write all that he wanted and no more.[20]

Since all that the inspired authors or sacred writers assert must be considered as asserted by the Holy Spirit, one should affirm that the books of Scripture teach firmly, faithfully and without error the truth that God decided to put down in the sacred writings for our salvation's sake.[21] Thus, "every Scripture is divinely inspired and useful: it educates, it argues, it corrects, it teaches discipline, that the man of God may be perfect and instructed in every good deed" (2 Tim. 3, 16-17, Greek text).

---

17 Cf. Vatican Council I, *Constitutio dogmatica de fide catholica,* ch. 2 (*Denz.* 1787; 3006); Biblical Commission, Decree of June 18, 1915 (*Denz.* 2180; 3629; *Enchiridion Biblicum,* 420); Holy Office, Letter of Dec. 22, 1963 (*E.B.* 499).

18 Cf. Pius XII, Encyclical Letter *Divino afflante Spiritu,* Sept. 30, 1943 (*A.A.S.* 35 [1943], p. 314; *E.B.* 556).

19 On "*in* and *through* man", cf. Heb. 1, 1 and 4; 4, 7 (*in*); 2 Sam. 23, 2; Matt. 1, 22 and *passim* (*per*); Vatican Council I, *Schema de doctrina catholica,* note 9 (Coll. Lac., VII, 522).

20 Leo XIII, Encyclical Letter *Providentissimus Deus,* Nov. 18, 1893 (*Denz.* 1952; 3293; *E.B.* 125).

21 Cf. St. Augustine: *Gen. ad litt.* 2, 9, 20 (*P.L.* 34, 270-1); *Epistola 82,* 3 (*P.L.* 33, 277; *CSEL* 34, 2, p. 354); St. Thomas, *De veritate*, q. 12, a. 2, C; Council of Trent, session IV, *de canonicis scripturis* (*Denz.* 783; 1501); Leo XIII, Encyclical Letter *Providentissimus Deus* (*E.B.* 121, 124, 126-7); Pius XII, Encyclical Letter *Divino afflante Spiritu* (*E.B.* 539).

12. In Holy Scripture God spoke through men in a human way.[22] In order to discern what he wanted to communicate to us, the interpreter of Holy Scripture must carefully seek what the sacred writers truly meant and God gracefully revealed in their words.

Among other things, the "literary forms" are to be considered in order to find out the sacred writers' purpose. Truth is diversely presented and expressed in texts that are, in varying degrees, historical, prophetical, poetical, or belong to other forms of speech. Moreover, the interpreter ought to inquire into the meaning which, in his precise circumstances, the sacred writer intended to, and did, express, given the conditions of his time and culture and the nature of the literary forms then in use.[23] For, in order to understand what the sacred author wanted to say in writing, one has to take due account of the customary, indigenous ways of feeling, of speaking or of telling a tale, which obtained in the sacred author's times, and of those commonly used in human relations in that period.[24]

Scripture must be read and interpreted in the same Spirit in whom it was written.[25] To find out correctly the sense of the sacred texts, one must therefore consider with no less care the content and the unity of Scripture as a whole, paying attention to the living Tradition of the whole Church and to the analogy of faith. Exegetes are to work along

---

[22] St. Augustine: *De civitate Dei,* XVII, 6, 2 (*P.L.* 41, 537; *CSEL* XL, 2, 228).

[23] St. Augustine: *De doctrina Christiana,* III, 18, 26 (*P.L.* 34, 75-6).

[24] Pius XII, *loc cit.* (*Denz.* 2294; 3829-3830; *E.B.* 557-62).

[25] Cf. Benedict XV, Encyclical Letter *Spiritus Paraclitus,* Sept. 15, 1920 (*E.B.* 469); St. Jerome: *In Galat.* 5, 19-21 (*P.I.* 26, 417A).

those lines toward a deeper understanding and explanation of the meaning of Holy Scripture; and, thanks to this scholarly preparation, the Church's discernement will mature. For all these points concerning scriptural interpretation are ultimately subject to the Church's discernment: she fulfills the divine mandate and task of watching over and interpreting the Word of God.[26]

13. The wondrous descent of the eternal wisdom to our level is thus evident in Holy Scripture, while the truth and holiness of God are respected. "Thus we may learn the unutterable kindness of God, and how he adapted his speech, in his providence and care for our nature."[27] For the words of God, expressed in human tongues, became similar to human language, just as formerly the Word of the eternal Father, assuming flesh with its human weakness, became similar to man.

---

[26] Cf. Vatican Council I *Constitutio dogmatica de fide catholica,* ch. 2 (*Denz.* 1788; 3007).

[27] St. John Chrysostom, *In Genesim,* 3, 8 (hom. 17, 1) (*P.G.* 53, 134). *Attemperatio* [tr. as: "adapted his speech"] corresponds to the Greek word *synkatábasis.*

Study-Club Questions

1. How important is a knowledge of "literary forms" in biblical exegesis? Mention some literary forms found in the Bible.
2. In order to understand what the sacred author wanted to say in writing, one has to take due account of the customary, indigenous ways of feeling, of speaking or telling a tale, which obtained in the sacred author's times, and of those commonly used in human relations in that period. Is this also a worthwhile method for non-biblical exegesis?
3. Inspiration and the interpretation of Scripture go together in theology, as they primarily go together in the experience of those who are familiar with the spiritual reading of the Word of God. (a) What is biblical inspiration? (b) What is biblical interpretation?
4. Mention some important guidelines to be followed by exegetes, theologians, and preachers in their function of translating the Bible in the language of contemporary man?
5. What does Pius XII's encyclical *Divino afflante Spiritu* tell us about the problem of biblical exegesis? What does the Instruction *Sancta Mater Ecclesia* of the Biblical Commission (May, 1964) tell us of the historical value of the New Testament?
6. Inerrancy is a consequence of, yet cannot be equated with, inspiration. (a) What is biblical inerrancy? (b) How is it related to biblical inspiration?
7. To find out correctly the sense of the sacred texts,

one must consider with no less care the content and the unity of Scripture as a whole, paying attention to the living Tradition of the whole Church and the analogy of faith. Explain.

8. What is hermeneutics? Mention and briefly discuss some of the major methodological problems in the interpretation of the Bible.
9. Briefly discuss the statement of St. Vincent of Lerins that the faith of the Church of Christ increases "in each man as in the whole Church, in the succession of periods and centuries, in understanding, knowledge and wisdom, although it does so according to its own nature, namely, in the same dogma, the same sense and the same doctrine".
10. Every book of the Bible has a divine author and a human author. (a) Briefly discuss the relationship between these two simultaneous authorships. (b) What is the basis for the canonicity of the Bible?
11. What does the encyclical *Providentissimus Deus* of Leo XIII tell us about the charism of inspiration?
12. Holy Scripture is free from errors as regards the truth of salvation, but not necessarily in merely philosophical or scientific matters. Why?
13. What should be the focus of theological reflection on inspiration?
14. Biblical interpretation goes further than the discovery of the literal or historical sense reached by scientific exegesis. The spiritual sense is also important. Explain.
15. Instead of presenting Scripture in the negative perspective of its freedom from error, the Constitution on Divine Revelation prefers to stress positively its teaching of the truth. How important is this method in your own private reading of the Bible?

CHAPTER IV

The Old Covenant

14. God, who in his love carefully planned and prepared the salvation of all mankind, chose for himself, by a unique decision, a People whom he would entrust with his promises. By a covenant with Abraham (cf. Gen. 15, 18) and, through Moses, with the People of Israel (cf. Ex. 24, 8), he revealed himself, in words and deeds, as the only true and living God to the People he had acquired. Thus, Israel was destined to discover by experience which were God's ways with men, to understand them more deeply and clearly day by day when God spoke through the prophets, and to spread their knowledge among the nations (cf. Ps. 21, 28-29; 95, 1-3; Is. 2, 1-4; Jer. 3, 17). The design of salvation, foretold, detailed and explained by the sacred authors, stands out, as God's true Word, in the books of the Old Covenant. For this reason these divinely inspired books keep their permanent value: "Whatever was written, was written for our instruction, that, through perseverance and with the help of the Scriptures, we may have hope" (Rom. 15, 4).

15. The order of the old covenant was structured, above all, so as to prepare the advent of Christ, the universal redeemer, and his messianic kingdom, to announce him in prophecy (cf. Luke

24, 44; John 5, 39; 1 Pet. 1, 10), and to show him through various images (cf. 1 Cor. 10, 11). In ways adapted to the state of mankind before the time when Christ initiated salvation, the books of the Old Covenant reveal to all the knowledge of God and of man and the ways in which the just and merciful God deals with men. Although they also contain imperfect and provisional elements, these books nevertheless describe the true divine pedagogy.[28] They are to be received with devotion by the Christian faithful. For they express a true awareness of God. Splendid teachings about him, a healthy wisdom on matters of human life and admirable treasures of prayers are also stored up in them. Finally, the mystery of our salvation is enfolded in them.

16. God, the inspirer and author of the books of both Covenants, wisely caused the New to be latent in the Old, and the Old patent in the New.[29] Christ established the new covenant in his blood (cf. Luke 22, 20; 1 Cor. 11, 25); nonetheless, the books of the Old Covenant, assumed in their totality in the preaching of the Gospel,[30] acquire and manifest their full meaning in the new covenant (cf. Matt. 5, 17; Luke 24, 27; Rom. 16, 25-26; 2 Cor. 3, 14-16), which they in turn illustrate and explain.

---

[28] Pius XI, Encyclical Letter *Mit brennender Sorge,* March 14, 1937 (*A.A.S.* 29 [1937], p. 151).

[29] St. Augustine: *Quaestiones in Heptateuch* 2, 73 (*P.L.* 34, 623).

[30] St. Irenaeus: *Adversus Haereses,* III, 21, 3 (*P.G.* 7, 950); (=25, 1: Harvey 2, p. 115); St. Cyril of Jerusalem, *Catecheses* 4, 35 (*P.G.* 33, 497); Theodore of Mopsuestia, *In Soph.* 1, 4-6 (*P.G.* 66, 452D-453A).

Study-Club Questions

1. Who are the People of God? Why did God select such a Chosen People?
2. In ways adapted to the state of mankind before the time when Christ initiated salvation, the books of the Old Testament reveal to all the knowledge of God and of man and the ways in which the just and merciful God deals with men. Mention some Old Testament examples of God's dealings with men.
3. What is a covenant? Mention and briefly discuss some Old Testament covenants. What is the difference between the Old Covenant and the New Covenant?
4. The Old Testament reveals God through various images. Mention some of these images.
5. Why should the books of the Old Testament be received and read with devotion by Christians?
6. How can the Old Testament be patent in the New? How can the New Testament be latent in the Old?
7. The Old Testament reveals something essential to the Christian belief in the unity of God. Explain.
8. How does the Old Testament show the profound penetration of the Church in the "stuff" of mankind?
9. The Old Testament embodied the patriarchal and prophetic tradition of the Mosaic covenant. (a) What is the Mosaic covenant? (b) How important is it today in the life of the Church?
10. In the Old Testament various prophecies of the coming of the Savior are recorded. Mention some of them.

11. What is the basic religious attitude of the People of the Old Testament?
12. Why is Scripture the "soul of sacred theology"?
13. How can the reading of Scripture initiate a dialogue between God and man?
14. What does Romans 15, 4 tell us about the permanent value of Scripture?
15. Briefly discuss the covenant with Abraham mentioned in Genesis 15. How important was it for the history of salvation?

CHAPTER V

The New Covenant

17. The Word of God is God's saving power for all believers (cf. Rom. 1, 16). It is manifest and efficacious most of all in the books of the New Covenant. For, when the fullness of time had come (cf. Gal. 4, 4), the Word was made flesh and dwelt among us, full of grace and of truth (cf. John 1, 14). Christ inaugurated the kingdom of God on earth; by his actions and his words he showed his Father and himself; he completed his work in his death, his resurrection and his glorious ascension and in the sending of the Holy Spirit. Being raised above the earth, he who alone has the words of eternal life (cf. John 6, 68) draws all men to himself (cf. John 12, 32, Greek text). This mystery was not unveiled to other generations as it has now been revealed in the Spirit (cf. Eph. 3, 4-6, Greek text) to the holy apostles and prophets so that these might preach the Gospel, awake faith in Jesus, the Christ and Lord, and gather the Church together. The writings of the New Covenant subsist as a permanent and divine record of these facts.

18. Everybody knows that the Gospels rightly stand out among all the Scriptures, even those of the New Covenant. For they are the main record of the life and teaching of the Word incarnate, our Savior.

Always and everywhere the Church has taught, as she does now, the apostolic origin of the four Gospels. What the apostles preached on Christ's order, they and some apostolic men, under the Holy Spirit's influx, later transmitted to us in writing: this is the foundation of the faith, the fourfold Gospel according to Matthew, Mark, Luke and John.[31]

19. Our holy Mother the Church has firmly and constantly taught, as she does now, that these four Gospels, whose historicity she affirms without hesitancy, faithfully report what Jesus, the Son of God, in the course of his life among men actually did and taught until the day of his ascension for their eternal salvation (cf. Acts 1, 1-2). Indeed, after the Lord's ascension, the apostles reported to their audiences the things which he had said and done, with the fuller insight which they enjoyed,[32] once they had learned from Christ's glorious destiny and they were enlightened by the Spirit of truth.[33] Sacred authors wrote the four Gospels: some things they sorted out from among many that were transmitted orally or already in writing; some they brought together into a synthesis or they interpreted in keeping with the state of the Churches; in brief, they preserved the style of proclamation in order always to share with us true and authentic records of Jesus.[34] Whether from their own memory and remembrance or on the witness of those who "saw him from the beginning and were ministers of the

---

[31] Cf. St. Irenaeus: *Adversus Haereses,* III, 11, 8 (*P.G.* 7, 885; Sagnard, ed., p. 194).

[32] John 2, 22; 12, 16; cf. 14, 26; 16, 12-13; 7, 39.

[33] Cf. John 14, 26; 16, 13.

[34] Cf. Biblical Commission, Instruction *Sancta Mater Ecclesia* (*A.A.S.* 56 [1964], p. 715).

Word", they wrote with the purpose that we might know the "truth" of the words which we have been taught (cf. Luke 1, 2-4).

20. Besides the four Gospels, the canon of the New Covenant also contains the letters of St. Paul and other apostolic writings composed under the Holy Spirit's inspiration. According to God's wise design, these confirm what relates to Christ the Lord; they make his genuine teaching better and better known; they announce the saving power of the divine work of Christ; they tell the story of the beginnings and the admirable spread of the Church; and they foretell her glorious consummation.

For, as he had promised (cf. Matt. 28, 20), Christ was present with his apostles, and he sent them the Paraclete, the Spirit, to lead them into the fullness of truth (cf. John 16, 13).

Study-Club Questions

1. The Word of God is manifest and efficacious most of all in the books of the Old Testament. Show how this is true.
2. Apart from the apostles, how much of an influence did the early Christian community have on the formation of the Gospels?
3. Why is there an imbalance of treatment in the Constitution between the four Gospels and the rest of the New Testament?
4. When was the New Covenant made between God and man?
5. How did Christ inaugurate the kingdom of God on earth (a) by his actions, (b) by his words?
6. Briefly discuss what is meant by the apostolic origin of the Gospels.
7. How many authors of the New Testament are there?
8. How important are the New Testament epistles?
9. How many kinds of literary forms can you discover in the New Testament?
10. How did the apostles awaken faith in Christ and gather the Church together? How might you awaken faith in Christ and help to gather the Church together?
11. Why are there four Gospels in the New Testament? Can you mention any major differences among the four Gospels?
12. How does one enter the "ark of salvation" and become a member of the household of God?

13. Mention and briefly discuss the existential exegesis of Bultmann and the "post-Bultmannians". Carried to its extreme, how would this tendency ruin the Catholic conception of the Word of God as actually present in the reading of Scriptures?
14. In the Epistle to the Romans, chapters 1-3, what does St. Paul say about the Word of God being "God's saving power for all believers"?
15. How do the Epistles of St. John (a) confirm what relates to Christ the Lord, (b) make his genuine teaching better known, (c) and announce the saving power of the divine work of Christ?

CHAPTER VI

Holy Scripture in the Church's Life

21. The Church has always venerated the divine Scriptures like the Lord's body itself. Especially in the sacred liturgy, she never stops taking the bread of life from the table which is both that of the Word of God and that of the body of Christ, and offering it to the faithful. She has always considered them, as she does now, together with Holy Tradition, as the supreme rule of her faith. For having been inspired by God and set to writing once for all, they unfailingly communicate the Word of God himself, and they embody the voice of the Holy Spirit in the words of the prophets and apostles. Like the Christian religion itself, all Church proclamation must feed on, and be ruled by, holy Scripture. In the sacred books, the Father who is in heaven lovingly approaches his children and talks to them. The Word of God contains such force and efficacy that it stands out for the Church as nourishment and health and, for the Church's children, as strength of their faith, food for their soul, pure and perennial font of their spiritual life. These sayings apply excellently to Holy Scripture: "The Word of God is alive and active" (Heb. 4, 12); "it has the power of building up and sharing the heritage among all the saints" (Acts 20, 32; cf. 1 Thess. 2, 13).

22. Access to Holy Scripture must be wide open to the Christian faithful. For this purpose the Church at the beginning already received as her own the old Greek translation known as the *Septuagint*. The Church also always honors the other Oriental translations and the Latin translations, and first of all the one called the *Vulgate*. Since God's Word must be available at all times, the Church's maternal care sees to it that opportune and correct translations, especially from the original texts of the sacred books, are printed. If, at the appropriate occasion and with the approval of the Church's authority, they are prepared jointly with separated brethren, all Christians will be able to use them.

23. The bride of the incarnate Word, the Church taught by the Holy Spirit, endeavors to reach a deeper understanding of the Holy Scriptures in order always to feed her children with divine utterances. She therefore duly fosters the study of the holy Fathers of both East and West and of sacred liturgies. Catholic exegetes and the other students of sacred theology should zealously unite their efforts and, under the vigilance of the sacred magisterium, work at the investigation of the sacred letters with appropriate means. Their aim should be that as many ministers of the divine Word as possible may fruitfully provide the People of God with the nourishment of the Scriptures: it will enlighten the minds, strengthen the wills and attract the hearts of men to the love of God.[35] This sacred Synod encourages the Church's children who labor in the

---

[35] Cf. Pius XII, Encyclical Letter *Divino afflante Spiritu* (*E.B.* 551, 553, 567); Biblical Commission, *Instructio de S. Scriptura in Clericorum Seminariis et Religiosorum Collegiis recte docenda*, March 13, 1950 (*A.A.S.* 42 [1950], pp. 495-505).

biblical field, that, renewing their strength every day, they may steadfastly pursue, according to the mind of the Church, the completion of the work happily begun.[36]

24. As upon a permanent foundation, sacred theology rests upon the written Word of God in unity with holy Tradition. In this Word it finds strong support and ever new youth as it examines in the light of faith all the truth hidden in the mystery of Christ. The Holy Scriptures contain the Word of God and, on account of their inspiration, they are the Word of God. Accordingly, the study of the sacred text should be, so to speak, the soul of sacred theology.[37] The ministry of the Word also —namely, pastoral preaching, catechetical teaching and all Christian instruction, in which the liturgical homily should occupy a privileged place—is fed healthily and thrives in holiness, thanks to the same Word of Scripture.

25. It is therefore necessary for all clerics, and first of all for priests and for those who are lawfully engaged in the ministry of the Word as deacons and catechists, to devote themselves to assiduous sacred reading and careful study of the Scriptures. Otherwise, someone who must dole out to the faithful in his care the abundant wealth of the divine Word, especially in the sacred liturgy, might become "exteriorly a vain preacher of God's Word, not being interiorly a hearer of it".[38] This holy Synod also insistently and particularly exhorts all the Christian faithful and, above all, the religious, to learn "the

---

[36] Cf. Pius XII, *ibid.* (*E.B.* 569).

[37] Cf. Leo XIII, Encyclical Letter *Providentissimus Deus* (*E.B.* 114); Benedict XV, Encyclical Letter *Spiritus Paraclitus* (*E.B.* 483).

[38] St. Augustine: *Sermon* 179, 1 (*P.L.* 38, 966).

eminent knowledge of Jesus Christ" (Phil. 3, 8) through frequent reading of the divine Scriptures. "For to ignore the Scriptures is to ignore Christ." [39] Let them therefore willingly approach the sacred text itself, through the sacred liturgy, which is filled with the divine Words, through pious reading, and through the appropriate organs and other helps which are fortunately multiplied everywhere in our days with the encouragement and assistance of the Church's pastors. Let them remember, however, that prayer should accompany Scripture reading for a conversation to take place between God and man; for "we speak with him when we pray, and we hear him when we read the divine maxims".[40]

It belongs to the bishops, "among whom the apostolic doctrine resides",[41] to prepare the faithful in their care, at the right time, to make proper use of the divine books, especially of those of the New Covenant and first of all the Gospels. This should be done through translations of the sacred texts, to which necessary explanations that should be truly sufficient are attached. Thus the Church's children will safely and fruitfully converse with the Scriptures and be steeped in their spirit.

Furthermore, let editions of Holy Scripture, with appropriate notes, be published also for the use of non-Christians to whose conditions they should be adapted. Both those who have pastoral functions

---

[39] St. Jerome: *Comment. in Isaiam,* Prol. (*P.L.* 24, 17); cf. Benedict XV: Encyclical Letter *Spiritus Paraclitus* (*E.B.* 475-80); Pius XII: Encyclical Letter *Divino afflante Spiritu* (*E.B.* 544).

[40] St. Ambrose: *De officiis ministrorum,* I, 20, 88 (*P.L.* 16, 50).

[41] St. Irenaeus: *Adversus Haereses,* IV, 32, 1 (*P.G.* 7, 1071); (=49, 2 Harvey 2, p. 255).

and Christians of whatever state should take care to distribute them wisely in any way possible.

26. Through reading and studying the sacred books, "the divine Word is spread and clarified" (cf. 2 Thess. 3, 1), and the treasury of revelation entrusted to the Church fills the hearts of men more and more. As the Church's life increases through continuous access to the eucharistic mystery, a new impetus to her spiritual life may also be expected from a greater veneration of the Word of God, which "remains forever" (Is. 40, 8; cf. 1 Pet. 1, 23-25).

* * *

Each and every point stated in this Constitution has satisfied the fathers of the sacred council. And we, by the authority bestowed on us by Christ, together with the venerable Fathers, approve it in the Holy Spirit, we decree it and we enact it; and we order the promulgation, to God's glory, of what has been enacted synodically.

Rome, in St. Peter's Basilica, November 18, 1965

Paul, Bishop of the Catholic Church
(The Fathers' signatures follow)

Study-Club Questions

1. Why must all Church proclamations be fed on, and ruled by, holy Scripture?
2. How can this chapter serve as a starting point for an opening of Catholic concern for (a) Scripture, (b) Tradition, (c) scriptural reading and preaching, (d) a broader interest in a theology of the Word?
3. What is the ultimate purpose of the Constitution on Divine Revelation?
4. How could a theology of the Word help Catholic thought to unloose its ties to Western culture and civilization, thereby making itself more ready to encounter world cultures and world religions?
5. The prologue and first chapter of the Constitution on the Sacred Liturgy explain the principles of a theology of the Word in the framework of the liturgical action. What is this framework?
6. Compare this chapter with the Constitution on the Sacred Liturgy, nn. 7 (on the presence of the Word who speaks when the Scriptures are read in the liturgical assembly), 24, 33, 35, 51, 52 (where principles of liturgical participation in regard to scriptural readings are explained, and practical norms of liturgical reforms determined).
7. Paragraph 12 of the Constitution on the Church, which explains the "sense of faith" and the charism of the Christian people, is relevant to a theology of the development of doctrine (Constitution on Divine Revelation, n. 8). How do these two articles complement each other?

8. Chapter VII (Constitution on the Church), on the eschatological vocation of Christians, should be read in the perspective of the last chapter of the Constitution on Divine Revelation: a pastoral reevaluation of Scripture reading is bound to make the faithful much more aware of their heavenly citizenship and of their transitory status and pilgrim state in this world. Explain.
9. How does this Constitution constitute a great step forward toward an ecumenical consensus?
10. Briefly discuss the importance of Scripture reading for (a) priests, (b) religious, (c) seminarians, (d) lay people.
11. How many official texts of the Bible are there? Why should modern translations of the Bible, adapted to the vernacular, be made mainly on the original texts?
12. How can a study of the Fathers of the East and West help us to reach a deeper understanding of Scripture?
13. Why should editions of the Bible, with appropriate notes, be prepared for non-Christians?
14. How is the Word of God present in the liturgy?
15. How does sacred theology safeguard the deposit of faith?

Selected Bibliography

Chapter I:

Balthasar, Hans Urs von. *Word and Revelation.* New York: Herder & Herder, 1964.

Bulst, Werner. *Revelation.* New York: Sheed & Ward, 1965.

Rahner, Karl, and others. *The Word: Readings in Theology.* New York: P. J. Kenedy & Sons, 1964.

Semmelroth, Otto. *The Preaching Word.* New York: Herder & Herder, 1965.

Chapter II:

Moran, Gabriel. *Scripture and Tradition: A Survey of the Controversy.* New York: Herder & Herder, 1963.

Tavard, George. *Holy Writ or Holy Church.* New York: Harper, 1959.

Vawter, Bruce. *The Bible in the Church.* New York: Sheed & Ward, 1959.

Chapter III:

Daniel-Rops, Henri. *What Is the Bible?* New York: Hawthorn Books, Inc., 1958.

Levie, Jean. *The Bible, Word of God in Words of Men.* New York: P. J. Kenedy & Sons, 1958.

Schökel, Luis A. *The Inspired Word.* New York: Herder & Herder, 1965.

Steinmann, Jean. *Biblical Criticism.* New York: Hawthorn Books, Inc., 1958.

Chapter IV:

Flanagan, Neal. *Salvation History.* New York: Sheed & Ward, 1964.

McKenzie, John L. *The Two-Edged Sword.* Milwaukee, Wis.: Bruce Publishing Co., 1956.

McKenzie, R. A. F. *Faith and History in the Old Testament.* University of Minnesota, 1963.

Chapter V:

Auzou, Georges. *The Word of God.* St. Louis, Mo.: B. Herder Book Co., 1960.

Bouyer, Louis. *The Meaning of Sacred Scripture.* University of Notre Dame 1958.

Schnackenburg, Rudolf. *New Testament Theology Today.* New York: Herder & Herder, 1963.

Chapter VI:

Charlier, Celestin. *The Christian Approach to the Bible.* Westminster, Md.: Newman Press, 1958.

Danielou, Jean. *The Bible and the Liturgy.* University of Notre Dame, 1956.

Swidler, Leonard, ed. *Scripture and Ecumenism.* Duquesne University Press, 1965.

Tavard, George. *Theology of the Word.* New York: Paulist Press, 1963.